SCAN ME!
FOR DIGITAL CONTENT

The WORLD Around Us 3

An Integrated Science, Social Studies and Environmental Studies Book

To access digital content, please log in to **http://scholastic.co.in/en/products/twau/grade-3/sign-up**

Illustrations by Priyankar Gupta, Amit Vachharajani, Partha Sengupta, Priya Kuriyan, Vinayak Verma
Maps not according to scale

Images: Shutterstock unless specified

Published by Scholastic India Pvt. Ltd.
A subsidiary of Scholastic Inc., New York, 10012 (USA).
Publishers since 1920, with international operations in Canada, Australia, New Zealand, the United Kingdom, India, and Hong Kong.

This edition: 2026

ISBN-13: 978-81-8477-369-9

Printed at : Shiv Shakti Printing & Trading Co., Haryana

Contents

Introduction

The World Around Us is a series of comprehensive environmental education course books for classes 1 to 5.

The books look at the child's natural, physical, and social environment. Within each level, lessons provide information from which basic concepts are deduced along with sufficient factual data, experiences and encouragement to enable them to generalise rationally about the environment.

This newly revised series is in accordance with the National Curriculum Framework (NCF) for School Education 2023, which has been adopted by the CBSE, ICSE and major state educational boards. It takes into consideration the curricular goals, competencies, and learning outcomes as illustrated by the NCF 2023.

Various sections in the books have been tagged to illustrate how the learning material adheres to the various skills and approaches recommended by the Framework.

In keeping with the spirit of advancement of technology in the field of education, the books exemplify how the 21st Century Skills of Information Literacy, Learning and Social skills have been interwoven into various tasks. Various exercises give students practice in using the scientific ways of learning and also using art to acquire information and express opinions. Consistent with the NEP's holistic approach to teaching and learning, the books raise awareness towards adopting sustainable practices for the environment and encourage cooperation amongst peers and in the society through various group and pair work tasks. The books follow the student-centered method of learning through discovery which ensures that the students learn about and relate to the concepts rather than memorise them.

Skill development

21st Century Skills

Communication

The skill of communication is engaging with others and exchanging ideas. Persons fluent in this skill are able to express thoughts and ideas clearly and coherently.

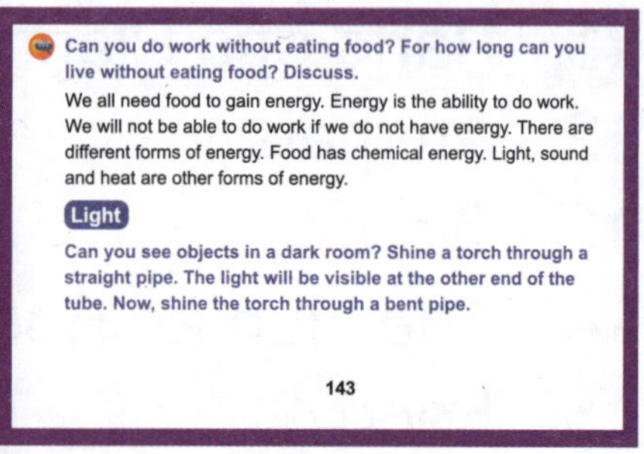

Can you do work without eating food? For how long can you live without eating food? Discuss.

We all need food to gain energy. Energy is the ability to do work. We will not be able to do work if we do not have energy. There are different forms of energy. Food has chemical energy. Light, sound and heat are other forms of energy.

Light

Can you see objects in a dark room? Shine a torch through a straight pipe. The light will be visible at the other end of the tube. Now, shine the torch through a bent pipe.

143

Creativity

It is the ability to use imagination and art, and think outside the box to solve problems for a more holistic understanding.

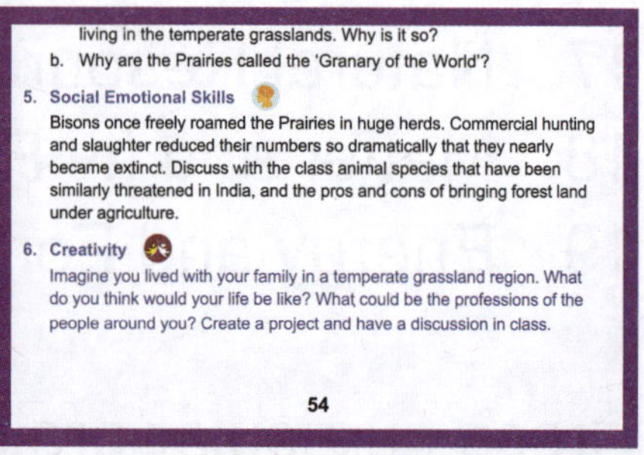

living in the temperate grasslands. Why is it so?

b. Why are the Prairies called the 'Granary of the World'?

5. **Social Emotional Skills**

Bisons once freely roamed the Prairies in huge herds. Commercial hunting and slaughter reduced their numbers so dramatically that they nearly became extinct. Discuss with the class animal species that have been similarly threatened in India, and the pros and cons of bringing forest land under agriculture.

6. **Creativity**

Imagine you lived with your family in a temperate grassland region. What do you think would your life be like? What could be the professions of the people around you? Create a project and have a discussion in class.

54

Critical thinking

It is the approach to analyse and use reasoning to solve problems.

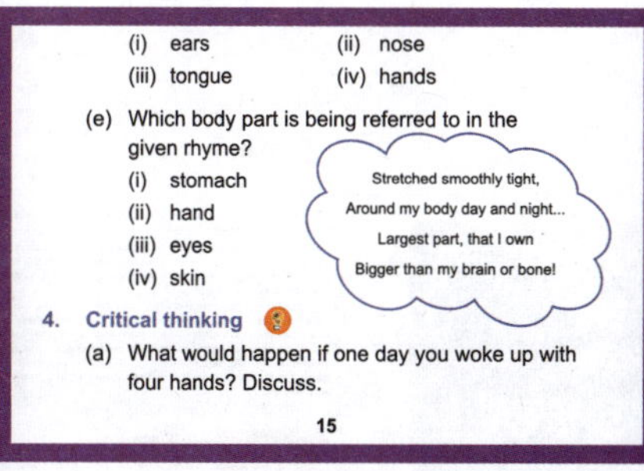

(i) ears (ii) nose
(iii) tongue (iv) hands

(e) Which body part is being referred to in the given rhyme?
(i) stomach
(ii) hand
(iii) eyes
(iv) skin

Stretched smoothly tight,
Around my body day and night...
Largest part, that I own
Bigger than my brain or bone!

4. **Critical thinking**
(a) What would happen if one day you woke up with four hands? Discuss.

15

Social emotional skills

These are a person's ability to connect with those around them. It spans across interaction with friends, family, peers, coworkers, etc.

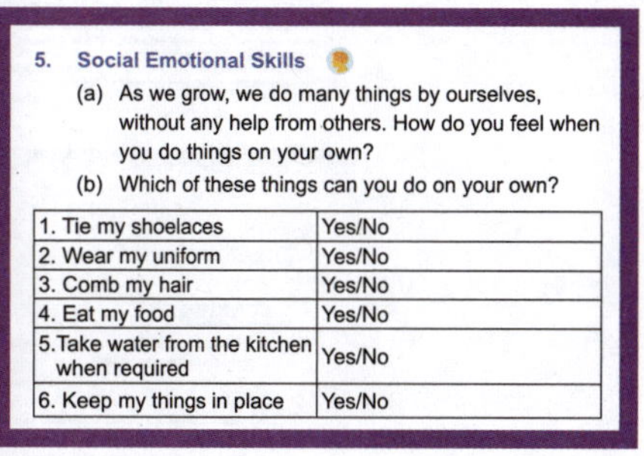

5. **Social Emotional Skills**
(a) As we grow, we do many things by ourselves, without any help from others. How do you feel when you do things on your own?
(b) Which of these things can you do on your own?

1. Tie my shoelaces	Yes/No
2. Wear my uniform	Yes/No
3. Comb my hair	Yes/No
4. Eat my food	Yes/No
5. Take water from the kitchen when required	Yes/No
6. Keep my things in place	Yes/No

Information literacy

These are a set of abilities required to recognise when information is needed and have the ability to locate, evaluate, and be able to effectively use the needed information.

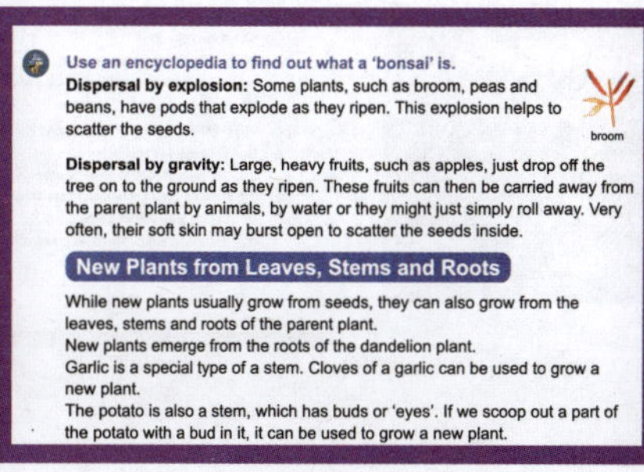

Use an encyclopedia to find out what a 'bonsai' is.

Dispersal by explosion: Some plants, such as broom, peas and beans, have pods that explode as they ripen. This explosion helps to scatter the seeds.

broom

Dispersal by gravity: Large, heavy fruits, such as apples, just drop off the tree on to the ground as they ripen. These fruits can then be carried away from the parent plant by animals, by water or they might just simply roll away. Very often, their soft skin may burst open to scatter the seeds inside.

New Plants from Leaves, Stems and Roots

While new plants usually grow from seeds, they can also grow from the leaves, stems and roots of the parent plant.
New plants emerge from the roots of the dandelion plant.
Garlic is a special type of a stem. Cloves of a garlic can be used to grow a new plant.
The potato is also a stem, which has buds or 'eyes'. If we scoop out a part of the potato with a bud in it, it can be used to grow a new plant.

The 21st century skills help us in dealing with today's challenges. Meanwhile, the Sustainable Development Goals (SDGs) are a global framework that can guide us towards a sustainable future.

Sustainable Development Goals

These were adopted by the United Nations in 2015 as a universal call to action to end poverty and protect the planet. The 17 SDGs recognise that action in one area will affect outcomes in others, and that development must balance social, economic and environmental sustainability.

Discovery-oriented & Activity-based Learning

The **Explore** section gauges prior knowledge as well as builds curiosity.

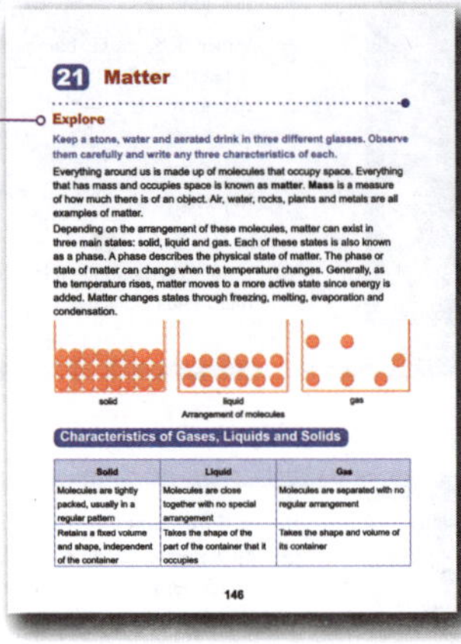
21 Matter

Explore

Keep a stone, water and aerated drink in three different glasses. Observe them carefully and write any three characteristics of each.

Everything around us is made up of molecules that occupy space. Everything that has mass and occupies space is known as matter. Mass is a measure of how much there is of an object. Air, water, rocks, plants and metals are all examples of matter.

Depending on the arrangement of these molecules, matter can exist in three main states: solid, liquid and gas. Each of these states is also known as a phase. A phase describes the physical state of matter. The phase or state of matter can change when the temperature changes. Generally, as the temperature rises, matter moves to a more active state since energy is added. Matter changes states through freezing, melting, evaporation and condensation.

Characteristics of Gases, Liquids and Solids

Solid	Liquid	Gas
Molecules are tightly packed, usually in a regular pattern	Molecules are close together with no special arrangement	Molecules are separated with no regular arrangement
Retains a fixed volume and shape, independent of the container	Takes the shape of the part of the container that it occupies	Takes the shape and volume of its container

146

The **Learn More** section acts as an important educational tool to develop independent and critical thinking skills.

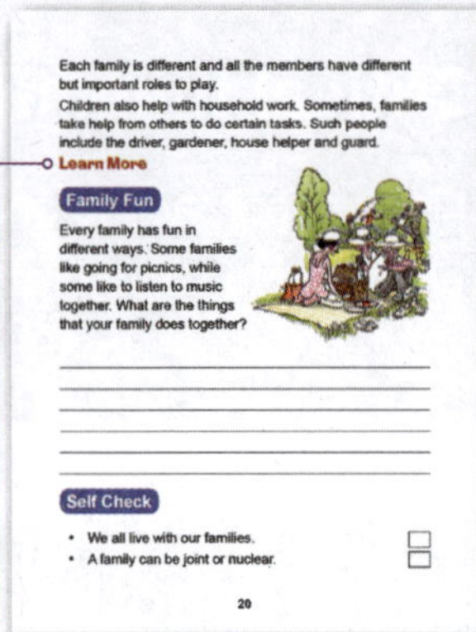
Each family is different and all the members have different but important roles to play.

Children also help with household work. Sometimes, families take help from others to do certain tasks. Such people include the driver, gardener, house helper and guard.

Learn More

Family Fun

Every family has fun in different ways. Some families like going for picnics, while some like to listen to music together. What are the things that your family does together?

Self Check

- We all live with our families.
- A family can be joint or nuclear.

20

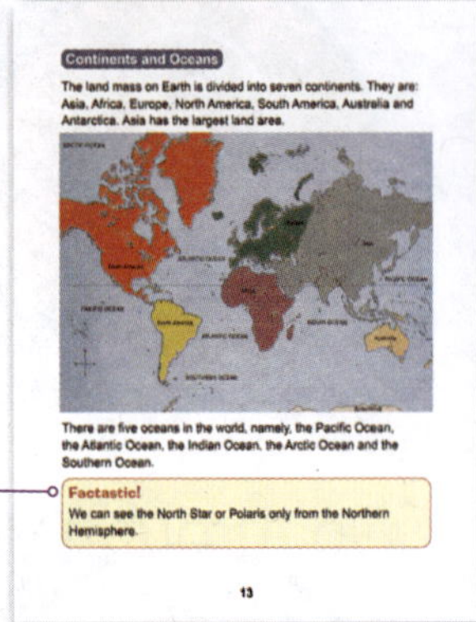
Continents and Oceans

The land mass on Earth is divided into seven continents. They are: Asia, Africa, Europe, North America, South America, Australia and Antarctica. Asia has the largest land area.

There are five oceans in the world, namely, the Pacific Ocean, the Atlantic Ocean, the Indian Ocean, the Arctic Ocean and the Southern Ocean.

Factastic!

We can see the North Star or Polaris only from the Northern Hemisphere.

13

Relevant, interesting nuggets of information are presented in an easy-to-understand format in the **Factastic** section.

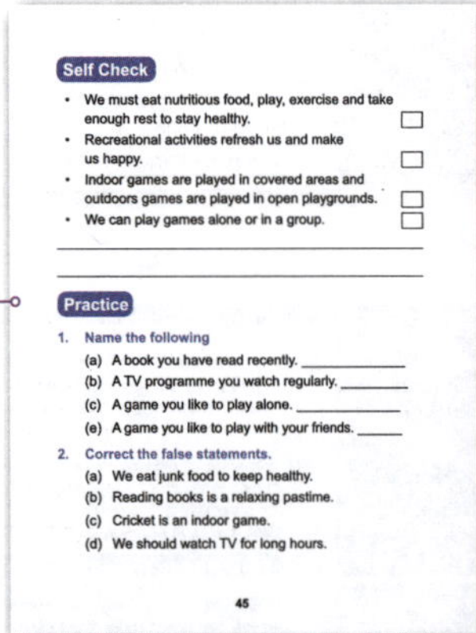
Self Check

- We must eat nutritious food, play, exercise and take enough rest to stay healthy.
- Recreational activities refresh us and make us happy.
- Indoor games are played in covered areas and outdoors games are played in open playgrounds.
- We can play games alone or in a group.

Practice

1. Name the following
   (a) A book you have read recently.
   (b) A TV programme you watch regularly.
   (c) A game you like to play alone.
   (e) A game you like to play with your friends.
2. Correct the false statements.
   (a) We eat junk food to keep healthy.
   (b) Reading books is a relaxing pastime.
   (c) Cricket is an indoor game.
   (d) We should watch TV for long hours.

45

Exercises after every lesson to **evaluate** the students' progress.

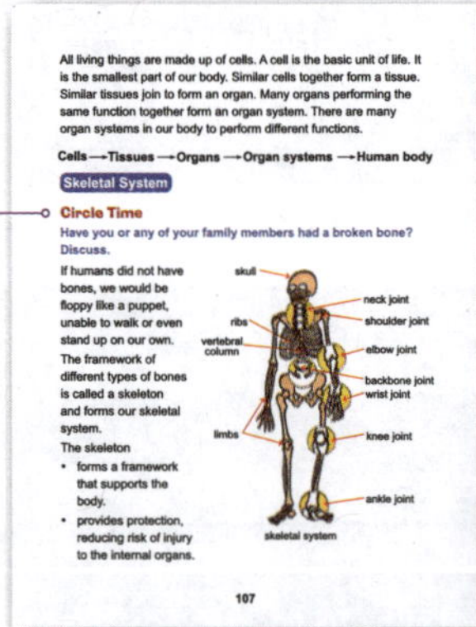
All living things are made up of cells. A cell is the basic unit of life. It is the smallest part of our body. Similar cells together form a tissue. Similar tissues join to form an organ. Many organs performing the same function together form an organ system. There are many organ systems in our body to perform different functions.

Cells → Tissues → Organs → Organ systems → Human body

Skeletal System

Circle Time

Have you or any of your family members had a broken bone? Discuss.

If humans did not have bones, we would be floppy like a puppet, unable to walk or even stand up on our own. The framework of different types of bones is called a skeleton and forms our skeletal system.

The skeleton

- forms a framework that supports the body.
- provides protection, reducing risk of injury to the internal organs.

107

The **Circle Time** section sets out peer and group activities which further promote exchange of ideas while also laying the foundation for teamwork and ethics.

Cross curricular project

Me and My Family

1. A family tree is a diagram that shows the relationship between many members of a family. Look at the family tree below. Paste pictures of your family members in the correct places.

Family Tree

Cross curricular projects offer a creative way of researching information, collaborating and expressing yourself on a common theme between different subjects.

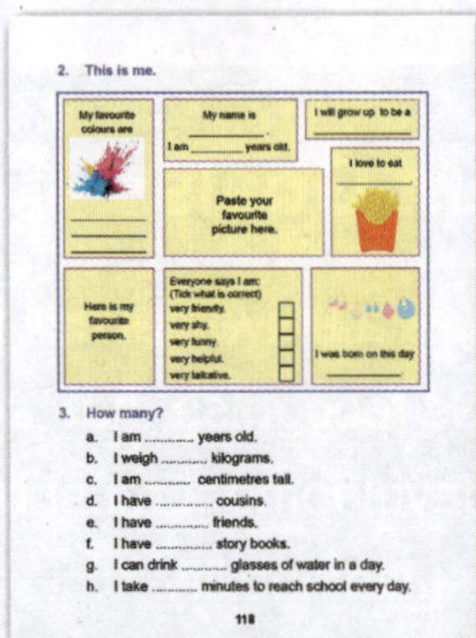
2. This is me.
3. How many?
   a. I am .... years old.
   b. I weigh .... kilograms.
   c. I am .... centimetres tall.
   d. I have .... cousins.
   e. I have .... friends.
   f. I have .... story books.
   g. I can drink .... glasses of water in a day.
   h. I take .... minutes to reach school every day.

118

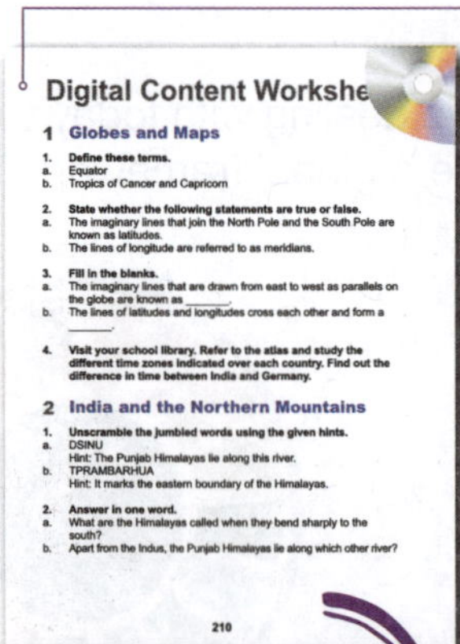
Digital Content Workshe

1 Globes and Maps

2 India and the Northern Mountains

210

Exercises based on the educative videos and animations in the **Digital Content** to extend learning.

Scan me

1 The Beginning of Time

Explore

Collect pictures of your family members and make a family tree.

Go through your old family photographs. Look for pictures of yourself as a baby. Also look for photographs of your parents, grandparents and other relatives when they were younger.

Your family as you see it today was not always like this. Your parents were once children, just like you are now. Your grandparents were once young, just like your parents are now. In the same way, the town you live in and the world around you were different in the past. Everything has changed and developed over time.

Try and find other sources that tell you about your family's history. Some families have pieces of jewellery, books or items of clothing that have been passed on from one generation to the next. These provide valuable information about a family's history.

Just as every family has a history, the human family, which has evolved over many thousands of years, also has a history.

Historians use information that they gather from studying **manuscripts**, coins, seals, remains of buildings & palaces, utensils, weapons, paintings, clothes and tools of the past as clues to put together a picture of what happened in the past.

Timelines

In order to understand the past, we need to know what happened in the past and when. Hence, it is essential to understand timelines, or the **sequence of events**.

historians: people who study history

sequence of events: the order in which events appear or occur

manuscripts: books written by hand

In order to understand the events that happened many, many years ago, historians have devised a special system of counting the years. The year of the birth of Jesus Christ is taken to be year zero. We begin our calendar from year 1. So, the first year after Christ was born is written as 1 CE (where CE stands for Christian Era or Common Era).

We are currently in 20 _____ CE, which is 20 ____ years after Jesus's birth.

But time existed even before the birth of Christ. So how is that time measured? Historians came up with a plan to count the time before the birth of Christ by counting backwards from the year zero. So, the year just before Christ was born is written as 1 BCE (where BCE stands for Before Christian Era/Before Common Era). When we say that the Great Pyramids were built in 2550 BCE, we mean that they were built 2,550 years before the birth of Christ.

> **Factastic!**
> The terms CE and BCE came into use very recently. Earlier, the terms used were BC (Before Christ) and AD (Anno Domini).

a timeline

Early Humans

The human family evolved many years ago. Early humans were called hominids. They used tools for hunting, lived in caves and forests, and moved from place to place in small groups in search of food. They covered themselves with leaves or skins of animals. These hominids evolved into early human beings or *Homo sapiens* about 195,000 years ago.

We have been able to find out about these early people from human remains found in Africa, cave paintings, remains of shelters and stone tools.

evolution of humans

Factastic!

The scientific name for human beings is *Homo sapiens*. Scientists believe that modern humans appeared about 180,000 years ago. They evolved over millions of years from many extinct species of apes.

Use an encyclopedia or search the Internet to find out when early humans first made homes in caves.

Tools

stone age tools

Gradually, early humans realised that they needed sharp tools to dig out roots and to kill animals for food. They started polishing and sharpening stones, bones and wood to make tools and weapons. They made better tools by striking one stone against another, till the stone developed a sharp edge. They hunted small animals and collected wild fruits and plants. They learnt to tie sharp stones to sticks and use them as spears to kill animals. This helped them hunt without getting too close to the animals they were hunting. They also learnt to make and use tools for fishing, digging and sewing. As many stone tools were used during this period, it is referred to as the **Stone Age**.

Early humans did not have a language of communication, so they used hand movements to talk to each other. However, as humans started to hunt, they started to imitate the calls of different animals. They used these sounds while hunting and when communicating with each other.

Early humans also discovered that they could stay warm and protect their bodies by wearing the fur and skin of animals. These were their first clothes. They gradually learnt to use stone tools to roughly sew together pieces of fur, animal skins and leaves to make clothes.

Discovering Fire

Early humans would often see fires breaking out in forests. They soon realised that fire kept away the cold as well as wild animals. They discovered that they could make fire by rubbing together two stones or sticks. This was a great discovery and it brought about many changes in their lifestyle. They realised that they could keep a fire burning by adding dry leaves and twigs to it. Early humans accidentally discovered that fire could be used to cook food, too. They discovered that food tasted better when cooked.

Settling Down

As early humans wandered from one place to another, they observed plants growing in the wild. They discovered that whenever they threw away the seeds of the fruits they ate, new plants grew from those seeds. They soon discovered that they could grow their own food and no longer needed to move from place to place in search of food. This is how farming began.

As they started to grow their own food, they had to settle down in one place in order to look after the plants. They chose areas near rivers, where the land was suitable for farming. Humans now began to grow more food than they required. They thus had to find ways of storing this extra food.

As early humans started to settle down, they began to live as a community. While some people hunted wild animals, others took up farming. Some made pots that were used for storing surplus grains and, perhaps, water. They also began to build houses to live in. This led to the formation of a settlement or a village.

Later, they started to rear animals, such as pigs, goats and sheep, to provide them with meat and milk. Cows were tamed and used in farming as well.

Visit a museum or watch a documentary based on early human life.

Transportation

Early humans had to walk long distances and carry heavy loads. As they settled down, they learnt that some animals could be tamed and used for carrying loads and ploughing land. Animals made it easier for humans to transport goods.

Soon, early humans learnt to tie logs together to make rafts that allowed them to travel and carry heavy loads by river. But travelling and transporting heavy loads by land was still very difficult. They made sledges or carts that could be pulled along the ground. They pushed and pulled heavy loads on these sledges. They also used animals to pull the sledges, but this was not easy. The sledges could move only where the ground was smooth.

Invention of the Wheel

Early humans observed that it was easy to roll down logs from a hilltop. They realised that round things could move easily. So, humans fitted their sledges with pieces of tree trunks so that they could roll. Thus, the wheel was invented.

The invention of the wheel improved the quality of life of early humans. Travel by land became much easier. It was now possible to transport stone boulders to build permanent houses. The invention of the wheel was a turning point for humankind.

Discovery of Metals

Humans discovered that when some stones were heated, liquids oozed out of them that hardened on cooling. This is how early humans discovered metals such as copper and iron. These metals could be forged to make sharp and sturdy tools for farming and hunting. The metals were also used to make better wheels that improved transportation. The discovery of metals made the tools used by early humans very efficient.

Learn More

Have a class discussion on how life would have been different for humans if the wheel had never been invented.

Self Check

- The world around us has changed and developed over time. ☐
- The year of the birth of Jesus Christ is taken as year zero, the starting point. ☐
- The year before Christ was born is written as 1 BCE. ☐
- The year after Christ was born is written as 1 CE. ☐
- Early humans did not have clothes to wear and lived in caves. ☐
- Later, they learnt to grow plants, tame animals and make clothes from leaves or the skins of animals. ☐
- Early humans discovered how to make fire by striking one stone against another or by rubbing a stick against a piece of wood. ☐

- The invention of the wheel brought about many changes in the lifestyle of early humans. ☐

____

____

Practice

1. Use the clues in the brackets to unscramble these words.

a. SRIOTHY (the study of the past) ______________

b. AANRLECD (used to see the year/dates) ______________

c. IIEENMTL (the sequence of events) ______________

d. SEAVC (early humans lived here) ______________

e. IERF (used by early humans to stay warm and cook) ______________

f. EEHWL (its invention was the turning point in human history) ______________

2. Write T for true and F for false.

a. The earliest human remains have been found in Asia. ☐

b. The year of the birth of Jesus Christ is taken to be zero. ☐

c. The first year after Christ was born is written as 2 CE. ☐

d. The scientific name for human beings is *Homo sapiens*. ☐

e. Early humans used language to communicate with each other. ☐

f. Animals made it easier for humans to transport goods. ☐

3. Answer the following questions.

a. What is a timeline?

b. How do we measure the years before the birth of Jesus Christ?

c. What kinds of tools were used by early humans? What materials did they use to make these tools?

d. What did early humans use fire for? What do modern humans use fire for?

e. What would you do to save yourself from heat and cold if you were living in the Stone Age?

f. How has the invention of the wheel transformed human life?

4. Critical Thinking

a. Why did early humans use hand movements to communicate?

b. Why did early humans settle down?

5. Social Emotional Skills

Discuss how easy our lives are now, compared to the lives of early humans.

6. Creativity

Use soft clay to try and make the face of an early human.

2 Maps and Directions

Explore

Draw a sketch of the route you take from home to your school. Mark all the important landmarks that you see on the way.

A **map** is a drawing or a sketch of an area. A map can be of a small neighbourhood or it can show a large area or a country. Maps can be rough or accurate, depending on the use. There are various types of maps, like **political maps** and **physical maps**.
A book of maps is known as an **atlas**.

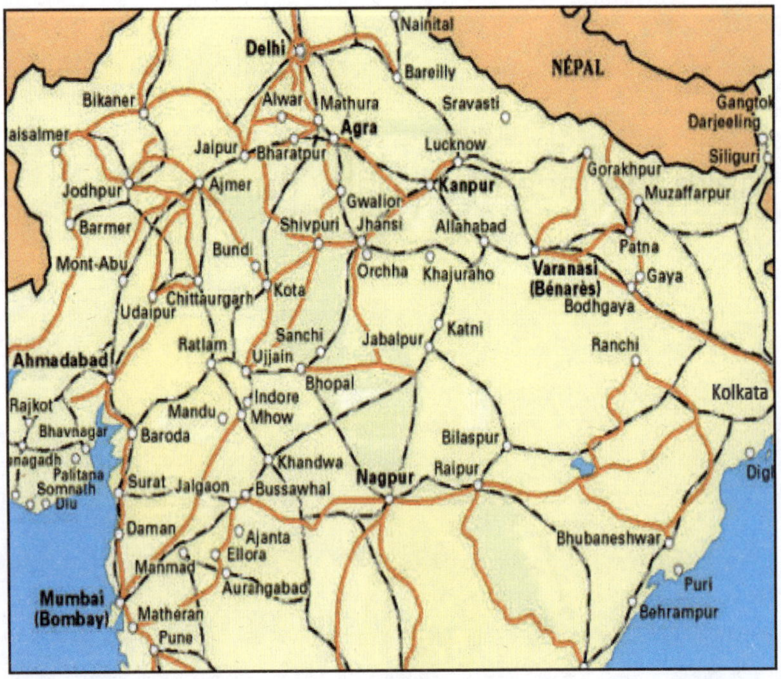

a map

What is a map?
A map is a drawing
To show us the way
To places near our town,
And those far away.
The red and black lines
Stand for highways we
take,
The blue wiggly lines
Are the rivers and
lakes.
The dots mark the cities
Where most people are,
The symbol for
a capital
Is a circle and star.

political maps: maps that depict man-made entities such as towns, cities, countries and roads

physical maps: maps that depict natural entities such as rivers, mountains, deserts and oceans

The **symbols** and **colours** on a map are used to show different things. **Legends** and **keys** help us to understand what each symbol stands for. The **scale** shows the relationship between actual distances and the distances on a map. For example, when we use a 1:1,00,000 scale, it means 1 cm on the map would be 1,00,000 kms in reality.

A model of the Earth is known as a **globe**. It shows us the Earth as a whole. We can rotate the globe to see the different places on Earth. The globe provides a very precise depiction of the Earth.

a globe

The **Equator** is an imaginary line on the globe which divides it into two equal hemispheres— northern hemisphere and southern hemisphere.

Locate your country on a globe as well as on a world map.

Directions

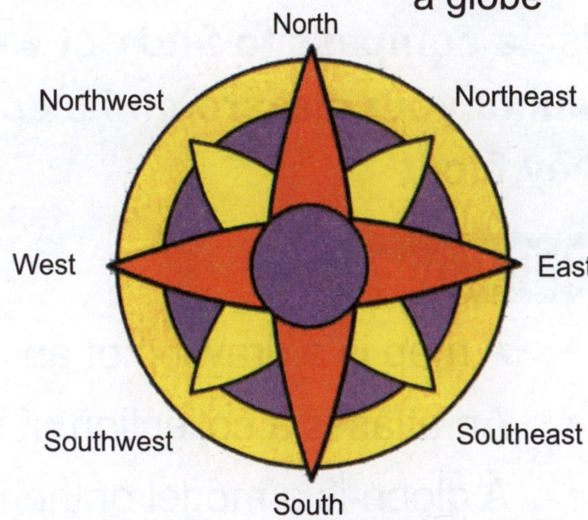

compass rose showing the main directions and sub-directions

Go to an open ground or park in the morning. Stand where you can see the Sun clearly. Remember, the Sun rises in the **East** and sets in the **West**. Now, stretch out your hands and point your right hand towards the Sun. Your right hand now points to the East. Your left hand points to the West. In front of you is **North** and behind you is **South**. These are the four main directions. Besides the four main directions or cardinal points, there are four sub-directions or intermediate directions. These are northeast (NE), northwest (NW), southeast (SE) and southwest (SW). The top of a map always indicates the North, while the bottom of a map always indicates the South. Find the positions of the sub-directions in the compass rose on page 16.

Factastic!

Early sailors studied the positions of the stars in the night sky and used the compass to navigate the seas. Even now, by studying the stars in the sky, sailors can determine their position and the route they need to take to reach their destination.

A compass is a navigational tool for finding directions. It consists of a magnetic pointer that moves freely and aligns itself to the Earth's magnetic poles. It always points to the Earth's Magnetic North.

compass

Learn More

Use a compass to find out which direction each wall of your classroom faces. Label the direction they face.

Self Check

- A map is a drawing of an area. ☐
- An atlas is a collection of maps. ☐
- A globe is a model of the Earth. ☐
- There are four main directions – North (N), South (S), East (E) and West (W). ☐
- The four sub-directions are – northeast (NE), northwest (NW), southeast (SE) and southwest (SW). ☐

____

____

Practice

1. Study the given map carefully.

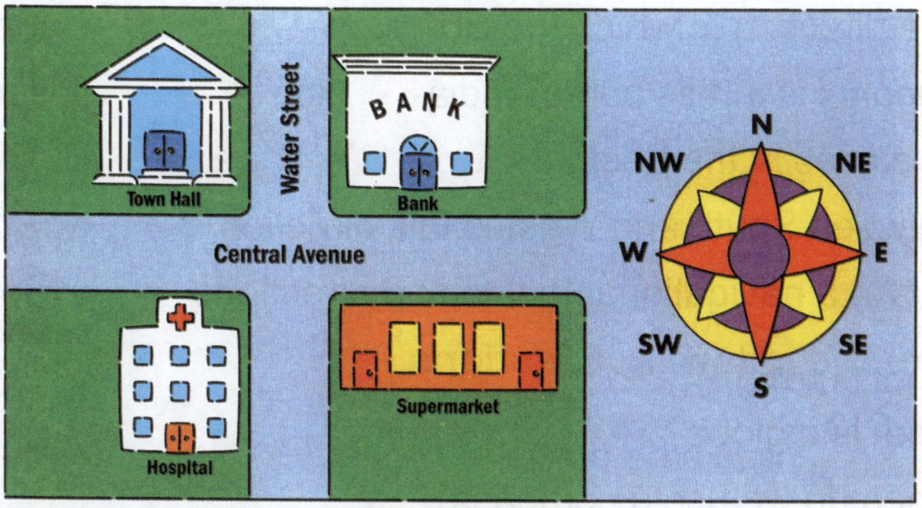

Now, colour each compass rose to show the correct direction.

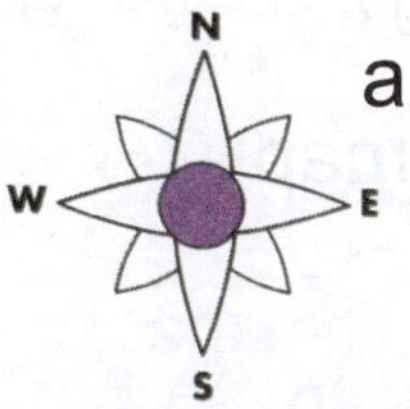

a. In what direction is the Town Hall from the Hospital?

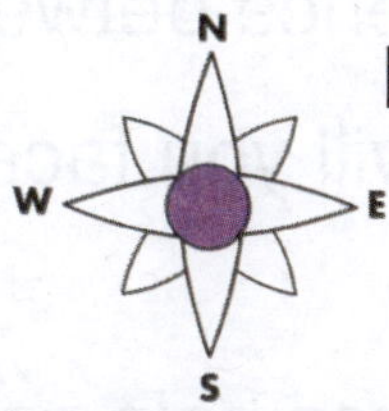

b. On which corner is the Supermarket?

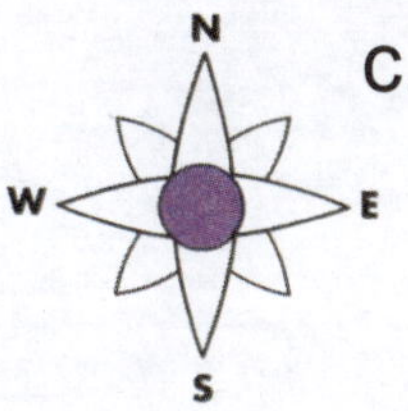

c. On which corner is the Hospital?

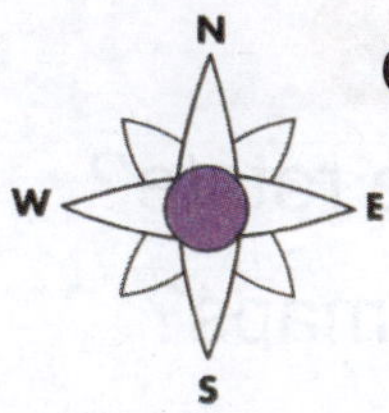

d. You ran out of money at the Supermarket. In which direction should you go if you need to get money from the Bank?

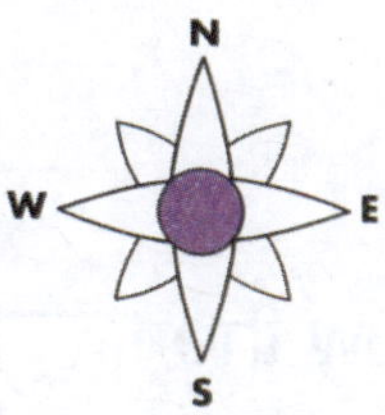

e. In which direction would you go if you wanted to go from the Supermarket to the Town Hall?

2. **Match the following.**

a. The direction in which the Sun sets	i. compass
b. Chennai is in this part of India	ii. south west
c. This rises in the East	iii. West
d. Between South and West is this direction	iv. Sun
e. This is a navigational tool to find directions	v. South

3. **Answer the following questions.**

   a. What is a globe?

   b. When do we use a compass?

   c. What is an atlas?

   d. What is the difference between a globe and a map?

   e. What difficulties will you face if you do not have a map while travelling?

   f. How can a compass help sailors who are lost at sea?

4. **Critical Thinking**

   a. Why does a globe rotate?

   b. Why do we need maps?

5. **Social Emotional Skills**

   Should we differentiate between people on the basis of the countries they live in? Discuss.

6. **Creativity**

   Draw a map of your school building on a chart paper. Show the locations and directions of the Library, Laboratory, Admin Office, Canteen and your classroom from the Principal's office.

3 Continents and Oceans

Explore

Find the names of any four countries that begin with the letter A. Locate them on a globe.

The surface of the Earth is covered by land as well as water.
Do you know how much of the Earth is covered by land and how much by water? Land makes up about one-fourth and water three-fourths of the Earth's total surface area.

The Shape of the Earth

The Earth seems endless and flat as you stand in an open field or at the seashore. In ancient times, people believed that if they travelled too far, they would fall off the edge of the Earth since they believed that the Earth was flat.

But is the Earth really flat? About 500 years ago, a Portuguese sailor, Ferdinand Magellan, set out with a fleet of ships from Spain. The fleet continued to sail in one direction for three years and ended up exactly where it had started. The fleet had actually sailed around the Earth. This proved that the Earth was round and not flat as previously believed.

Further proof that the Earth is round was provided when astronauts, people trained to travel into space, reported that the Earth looked like a huge ball from space.

The horizon is the circular line at which the sky and the Earth appear to meet. If we stand on a flat plain, the horizon appears to be at the same distance in every direction.

Oceans and Continents

Look at the map of the world. Some areas are coloured blue. The blue areas indicate water bodies and the other areas show land masses.

Very large land masses are known as **continents**. Very large water bodies are known as **oceans**.

continents and oceans

There are seven continents in the world. These are:

- Africa
- Asia
- Antarctica
- Australia
- Europe
- North America
- South America

Continents are further divided into smaller divisions. These are known as countries. India is part of the continent of Asia.

Factastic!

Australia is the smallest continent. Asia is the largest continent.

Circle Time

Play the word ladder game in class. Every student must come up with the name of an ocean, continent or country that starts with the same letter as the last letter of the word used by the student before him/her. For example, the ladder could be: Asia, Australia, Arctic Ocean, North America, etc.

Approximately 71 per cent of the Earth's surface is covered with water, which is divided into oceans and seas. An **ocean** is a large body of saline (salty) water.

There are five oceans in the world. These are:

- Arctic Ocean
- Atlantic Ocean
- Indian Ocean
- Pacific Ocean
- Southern Ocean

The Southern Ocean came to be recognised only in the year 2000. Earlier, this area was considered the southern part of the Atlantic, Pacific and Indian oceans.

Smaller bodies of water are known as **seas**. Oceans are very deep and are larger than seas. There are mountain ranges as well as trenches on the ocean floor. The **Mariana Trench**, located in the Pacific Ocean, is the deepest point on Earth.

Factastic!

The Southern Ocean is unique. All the other oceans are bordered by land on at least two sides. The Southern Ocean is the only ocean that does not have any land boundaries. Instead, it completely surrounds the continent of Antarctica.

An **island** is a piece of land that is surrounded by water on all sides. Very often, islands are the tops of underwater mountains. A group of islands located close to one another is called an **archipelago**.

Learn More

Use an atlas to find an archipelago in the Indian Ocean.

Self Check

- Land makes up about one-fourth and water about three-fourths of the Earth's total surface area. ☐
- Very large land masses are called continents. ☐
- Very large water bodies are called oceans. ☐
- There are seven continents and five oceans in the world. ☐

Practice

1. Find the names of the continents in the word grid.

x	y	z	x	y	u	b	c	d	g	i	a
n	o	r	t	h	a	m	e	r	i	c	a
z	u	w	a	v	x	e	f	h	i	j	k
l	p	q	n	c	d	a	f	r	i	c	a
o	m	r	t	e	q	z	e	b	c	a	u
t	s	n	a	x	z	m	d	e	f	r	s
u	x	z	r	y	a	s	e	i	h	q	t
u	v	q	c	h	s	r	u	j	g	p	r
a	c	w	t	l	i	q	r	m	n	o	a
d	b	u	i	k	a	p	o	t	k	l	l
f	o	e	c	j	m	o	p	x	s	v	i
s	g	h	a	i	m	f	e	y	w	u	a

2. Write T for true and F for false.

a. People always believed that the Earth was flat. ☐

b. Magellan set out with a fleet of ships from India. ☐

c. Magellan's sailors sailed around the Earth, proving that it was round. ☐

d. Our country is in the African continent. ☐

e. Australia is the smallest continent. ☐

3. Answer the following questions.

a. What is horizon?

b. How many oceans are there in the world? Name them.

c. Which continent is India a part of?

d. What is an archipelago?

e. What would happen if there were more continents and fewer oceans on Earth?

f. How advantageous is it for a country to be surrounded by seas?

4. Critical Thinking

a. Even if we travel very far, we will not fall off the edge of the Earth. Why?

b. Why does the horizon appear to be at the same distance in every direction?

5. Social Emotional Skills

The world is one family. Discuss.

6. Creativity

Take a world map. Colour and label the seven continents and cut them out. Make a globe using these cuttings and a big ball.

4 India—Physical

Explore

Find out which colours are used to show the following physical features on a map:

1. mountains 2. forests 3. rivers 4. deserts

India is a large country. There are deserts, thick jungles and long rivers in India. It has a long coastline and beautiful beaches. Some of the tallest mountains in the world are located in India.

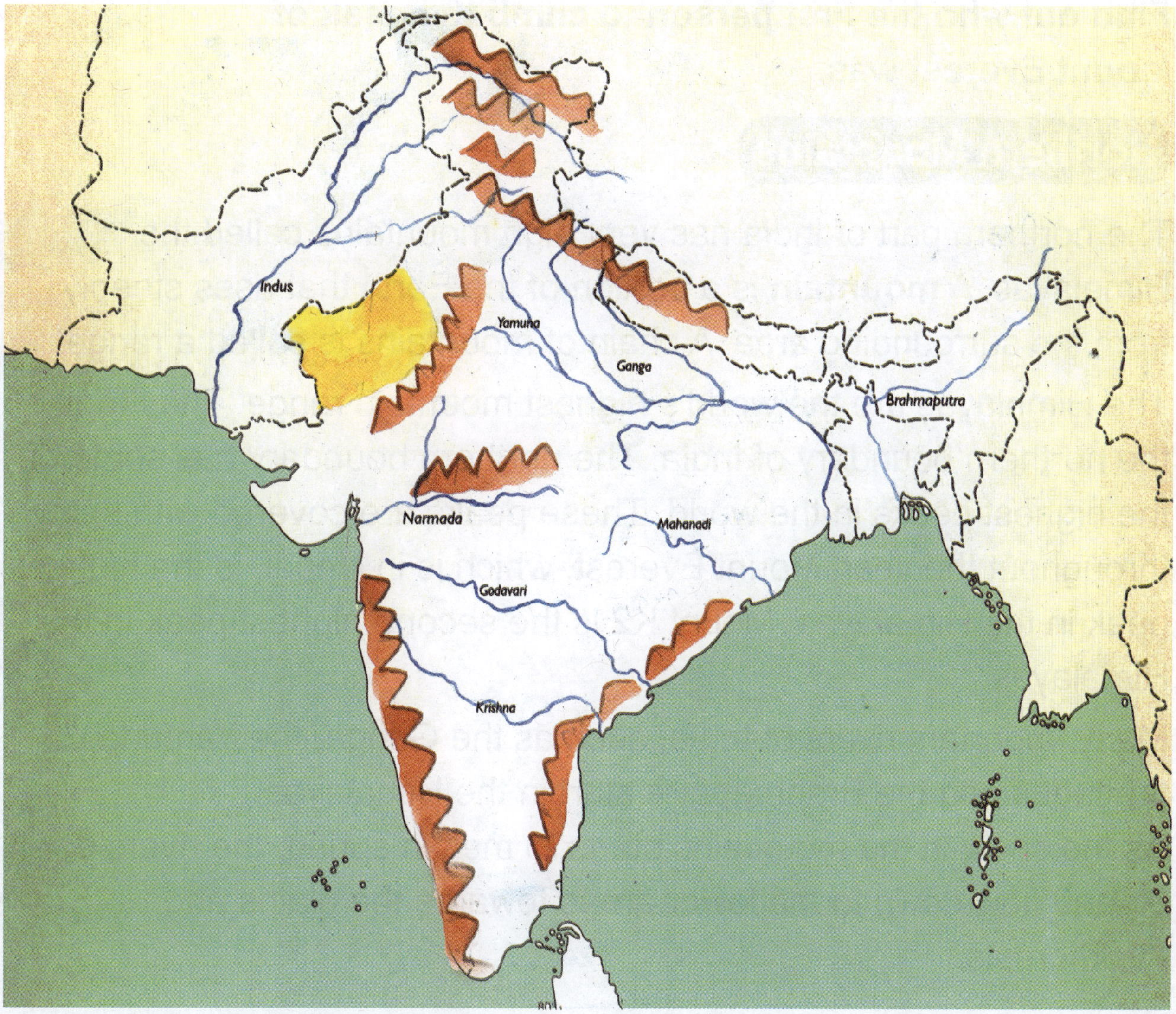

Factastic!

India is the seventh-largest country in the world. It is the most populated country in the world. China is the second most populated country in the world. Both China and India are located in the continent of Asia.

India can be broadly divided into six geographical regions. These are:

- the northern mountains
- the northern plains
- the desert region
- the Deccan plateau and the ghats
- the coastal region
- the islands

Find out who the first person to climb the peak of Mount Everest was.

Northern Mountains

The northern part of India has very high mountains called the Himalayas. A **mountain** is a portion of the Earth that rises steeply from the surrounding area. A chain of mountains is called a range.

The Himalayas are the world's highest mountain range. They form the northern boundary of India. The northern boundary has some of the highest peaks in the world. These peaks are covered with snow throughout the year. Mount Everest, which is in Nepal, is the highest peak in the Himalayas. Mount K2 is the second highest peak in the Himalayas.

Many important rivers of India, such as the Ganga, the Yamuna, the Indus and the Brahmaputra start in the Himalayas.

As the snow in the mountains starts to melt in spring, the rivers swell up and flow down to the lower areas towards the plains and thick forests.

This region, which has tall grass, is known as the **terai** region. Many animals live in the terai region, such as elephants, tigers, rhinoceros and deer.

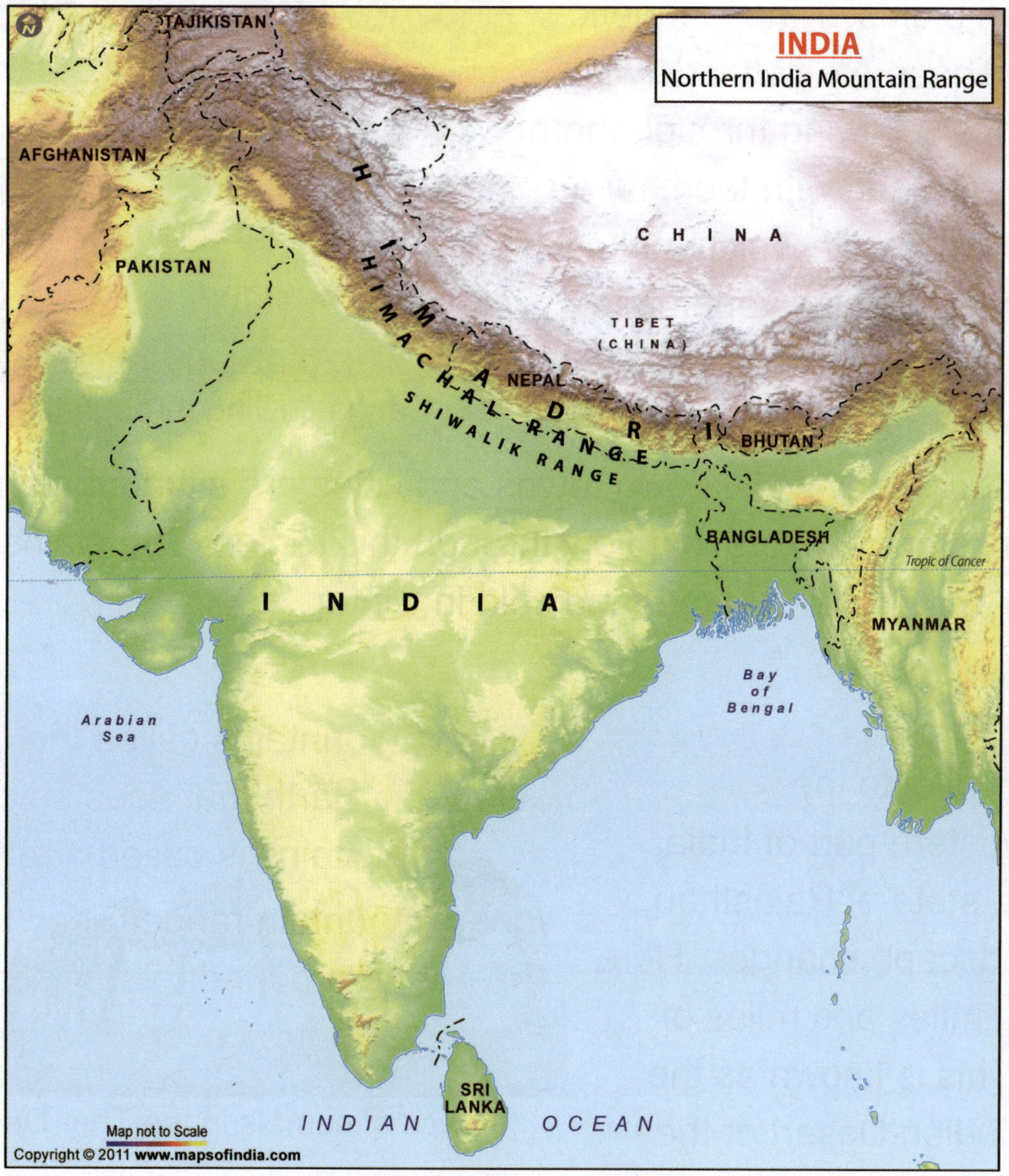

the northern mountains

Find out from where the River Ganga originates.

Northern Plains

South of the Himalayas are the northern plains or the Gangetic plains. These are flatlands with many rivers flowing through them. The rivers bring with them a fine soil known as silt, which makes the northern plains very fertile and most suitable for cultivation. The plains are very densely populated. Many well-known towns and cities are situated along the banks of the rivers that flow through this region. The plains are usually very hot in summer and cold in winter.

the Ganga flowing through the plains

Desert

As we travel to the northwestern part of India, into the state of Rajasthan, the landscape changes. Here we find miles and miles of sand. This is known as the Great Indian Desert or the Thar Desert. Since this region receives very little rainfall, hardly any crops grow here. This region experiences hot, dry summers and cold winters. The population in this region is very sparse as it is difficult to live in such extreme conditions.

a pack of camels in the Thar Desert

Factastic!

Villagers in Rajasthan depend on the camel as the main means of transport. Known as the ship of the desert, a camel can go without food and water for days together. It has wide cushioned feet that spread as it walks. This helps it to walk easily on sand without slipping. It also has two rows of eyelashes, and nostrils that can close completely. This prevents sand from entering the camel's eyes and nose.

Deccan Plateau and the Ghats

The southern part of India is a **peninsula**. A peninsula is a large piece of land thar juts out into the sea. It is surrounded by large water bodies on three sides. The Indian peninsula has the Bay of Bengal to the east, the Arabian Sea to the west and the Indian Ocean to the south.

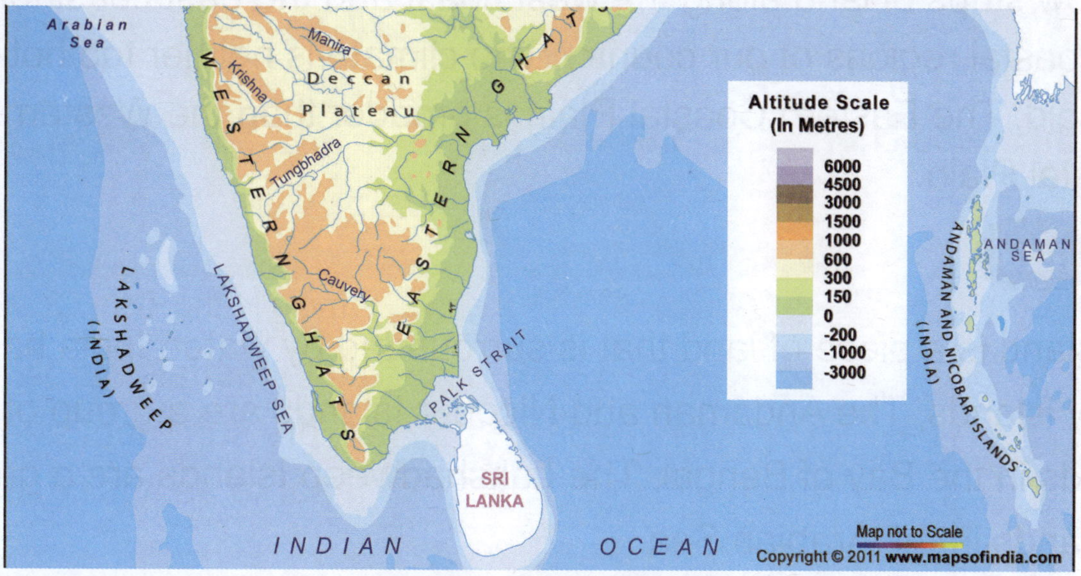

the Indian peninsula

This region of India is called the Deccan Plateau. A **plateau** is a raised portion of land that is flat on top.

The Deccan Plateau has many rivers, such as the Krishna, the Kaveri, the Godavari and the Mahanadi flowing through it. Unlike the rivers of the northern plains, the rivers in the Deccan Plateau are not snow fed. Instead, these are rain fed, that is, the source of water in these rivers is rain. The Deccan region is very rich in minerals. Some parts are covered by thick forests. The climate in the region is moderate, that is, it is neither too hot nor too cold.

Circle Time

Use an encyclopedia or the Internet to find out the difference between the Eastern Ghats and the Western Ghats. Present your findings in a chart and discuss.

Coastal Regions

The Deccan Plateau is bordered on the east by a range of mountains called the Eastern Ghats and on the west by a range of mountains called the Western Ghats.

Narrow strips of land along the west coast and the east coast form the coastal regions of our country. The climate is neither too hot nor too cold. The Eastern Coastal Plain is broader than the Western Coastal Plain.

Islands

An island is a piece of land that is surrounded by water. India has many islands. The Andaman and Nicobar Islands are a group of islands in the Bay of Bengal. The Lakshadweep Islands are a group of islands in the Arabian Sea.

Learn More

Use an atlas to find out the capital cities of the Andaman and Nicobar and Lakshadweep islands.

Self Check

- India is a large country with different physical features like deserts, mountains, forests and water bodies. ☐
- India is divided into six geographical regions: the northern mountains, the northern plains, the desert, the Deccan Plateau and the ghats, the coastal regions and the islands. ☐

____

____

Practice

1. Unscramble the letters to form words related to India's physical features.

a. YASMIHLAA ______________________

b. HTAR SDEETR ______________________

c. NWEETRS HGAST ______________________

d. RVRIE AGNGA ______________________

e. CADECN TEPLAUA ______________________

2. Write T for true and F for false.

a. In India, the highest peaks are found in the plateaus. ☐

b. The Indus river originates in the Himalayas. ☐

c. The eastern coastal plains are broader than the western coastal plains. ☐

d. The Andaman Islands are in the Bay of Bengal. ☐

e. The Thar Desert is very densely populated because of its easy living conditions. ☐

3. Answer the following questions.

a. What is a peninsula?

b. Name some rivers that start in the Himalayas.

c. Which three large water bodies surround India?

d. On a physical map of India, mark the following:

   i. The Thar Desert

   ii. The Himalayas

   iii. The Deccan Plateau

   iv. The Coastal regions

   v. The Andaman and Nicobar Islands

e. Describe the advantages of having the Himalayas as the northern boundary of India.

f. What is the source of water for rivers?

4. Critical Thinking

a. The Thar Desert is not very densely populated. Why is it so?

b. Why are the northern plains very fertile?

5. Social Emotional Skills

Why do we compare rivers to mothers? Discuss.

6. Creativity

Work in groups and create a poster displaying an advertisement for a holiday destination in the mountains or by the sea.

5 India—Political

Explore

Find the names of the countries with which India shares its boundaries. Locate them on a globe.

India is located in the southern part of the continent of Asia. India is surrounded by the Arabian Sea to the west, the Bay of Bengal to the east and the Indian Ocean to the south. Acting as a natural boundary, the Himalayas to the north separate India from the rest of the continent of Asia.

India—Neighbours

India shares its boundaries with many countries. Bangladesh and Myanmar lie to its east. Sri Lanka and the Maldives are to the south of India. Pakistan and Afghanistan are India's neighbours in the west. China, Nepal and Bhutan lie to the north of our country. India and its neighbours form the Indian **subcontinent**.

India and her neighbours

subcontinent: a large land mass that is part of a larger continent

Use an atlas to find out the capitals of India's neighbours.

India's Political Divisions

India is a very large country with a large population. The central or union government looks after the needs, welfare and safety of the people of our country. The central government is located in New Delhi, which is the capital city. The Prime Minister, the President and other ministers of the central government live in New Delhi.

Factastic!

People in India speak many different languages. About twenty-two regional languages are spoken in India.

As India is a large country, it is difficult for the central government to look after the needs of such a large population by itself. India has, therefore, been divided into twenty-eight states and eight union territories. Each state has a state government that looks after the well-being of all the people living in the state. The Governor, Chief Minister, other ministers and senior government officers of the state reside in the state capital.

Besides the states, there are eight union territories. These small areas come directly under the central government. Delhi is a union territory and is referred to as the National Capital Territory. The Andaman and Nicobar Islands form the largest union territory while Lakshadweep is the smallest. Hindi is one of our official language. The official languages of India are Hindi and English. The regional languages of the states are their respective official languages. People in different parts of the country have diverse ways of dressing and living and have diverse eating habits. But despite this diversity, there is a sense of unity among the people of our country.

India—states and union territories, and their capitals

List of States and Union Territories, and their Capitals

State	Capital
Andhra Pradesh	Amaravati
Arunachal Pradesh	Itanagar
Assam	Dispur
Bihar	Patna
Chhattisgarh	Raipur
Goa	Panaji
Gujarat	Gandhinagar
Haryana	Chandigarh
Himachal Pradesh	Shimla
Jharkhand	Ranchi
Karnataka	Bengaluru
Kerala	Thiruvananthapuram
Madhya Pradesh	Bhopal
Maharashtra	Mumbai
Manipur	Imphal
Meghalaya	Shillong
Mizoram	Aizawl
Nagaland	Kohima
Odisha	Bhubaneshwar
Punjab	Chandigarh
Rajasthan	Jaipur
Sikkim	Gangtok
Tamil Nadu	Chennai
Telangana	Hyderabad
Tripura	Agartala

State	Capital
Uttar Pradesh	Lucknow
Uttarakhand	Dehradun
West Bengal	Kolkata

Union Territory	Capital
Andaman and Nicobar Islands	Port Blair
Chandigarh	Chandigarh
Dadra and Nagar Haveli	Silvassa
Daman and Diu	Daman
Jammu and Kashmir	Srinagar (Summer), Jammu (Winter)
Ladakh	Leh
Lakshadweep	Kavaratti
Puducherry	Puducherry
National Capital Territory of Delhi (NCT)	New Delhi

Learn More

Where do you live? Write the name of your state/union territory, its capital city and the name of the Chief Minister.

Self Check

- India is located in the continent of Asia and is surrounded by the Arabian Sea, the Bay of Bengal and the Indian Ocean. ☐
- India has been divided into twenty-eight states and eight union territories. Each state has a state government and a regional language. ☐

Practice

1. Draw lines to match the states with their capitals.

State	Capital
a. Uttar Pradesh •	• Bhubaneshwar
b. Punjab •	• Kolkata
c. Goa •	• Bengaluru
d. Mizoram •	• Chandigarh
e. Karnataka •	• Lucknow
f. Odisha •	• Panaji
g. West Bengal •	• Aizawl

2. Fill in the blanks to complete the sentences.

a. India's national language is ________.

b. The __________ separate India from the rest of Asia.

c. India has _________ union territories.

d. India has _________ states.

e. India is located in the continent of _________.

3. Answer the following questions.

a. Name India's neighbours.

b. Name the largest and the smallest union territories in India.

c. Where is the central government located?

d. Label your state and its neighbouring states on a blank political map of India.

e. What is the difference between a state and a union territory?

f. It is an advantage that India is divided into states. Explain.

4. **Critical Thinking**

   a. The Himalayas are a natural boundary separating India from other countries. Explain.

   b. Why does India have many regional languages despite having two official languages?

5. **Social Emotional Skills**

   Find out different aspects of the culture of the state you belong to. Discuss in the class.

6. **Creativity**

   Which states will you travel across if you go from Delhi to Bengaluru by train? You can use the Internet or an atlas to find this information.

   Colour all these states on a blank political map of India.

6 India—Food and Clothing

Explore

What is the staple food of your state? Bring it in your lunch box and share.

India is a large country with diverse climatic and weather conditions. The food and clothes of Indians vary, depending on where they live.

Food

People across the country eat different kinds of food. The food that people eat in a particular region is known as the **staple food** of that region.

wheat

rice

The climate and the soil of a particular region influences the types of crops that can be grown there. For example, rice grows best in regions where there is ample rain. Thus, it will not grow well in Rajasthan where there is very little rainfall and the soil is very sandy. On the other hand, this type of soil is very good for growing wheat, *bajra* and *jowar*.

In the western and central parts of India, wheat, *bajra* and *jowar* are widely used.

In the northern parts of the country, wheat is preferred over rice. Rice is the staple food of people living in the eastern and southern parts of India. In the coastal regions of India, fish is widely eaten.

Pulses are also eaten throughout the country.

pulses

Fruits and vegetables are also a very important part of the Indian diet. Fruits and vegetables are available throughout the year. Fruits require very specific weather and soil conditions to grow. Different fruits, therefore, grow in different parts of the country.

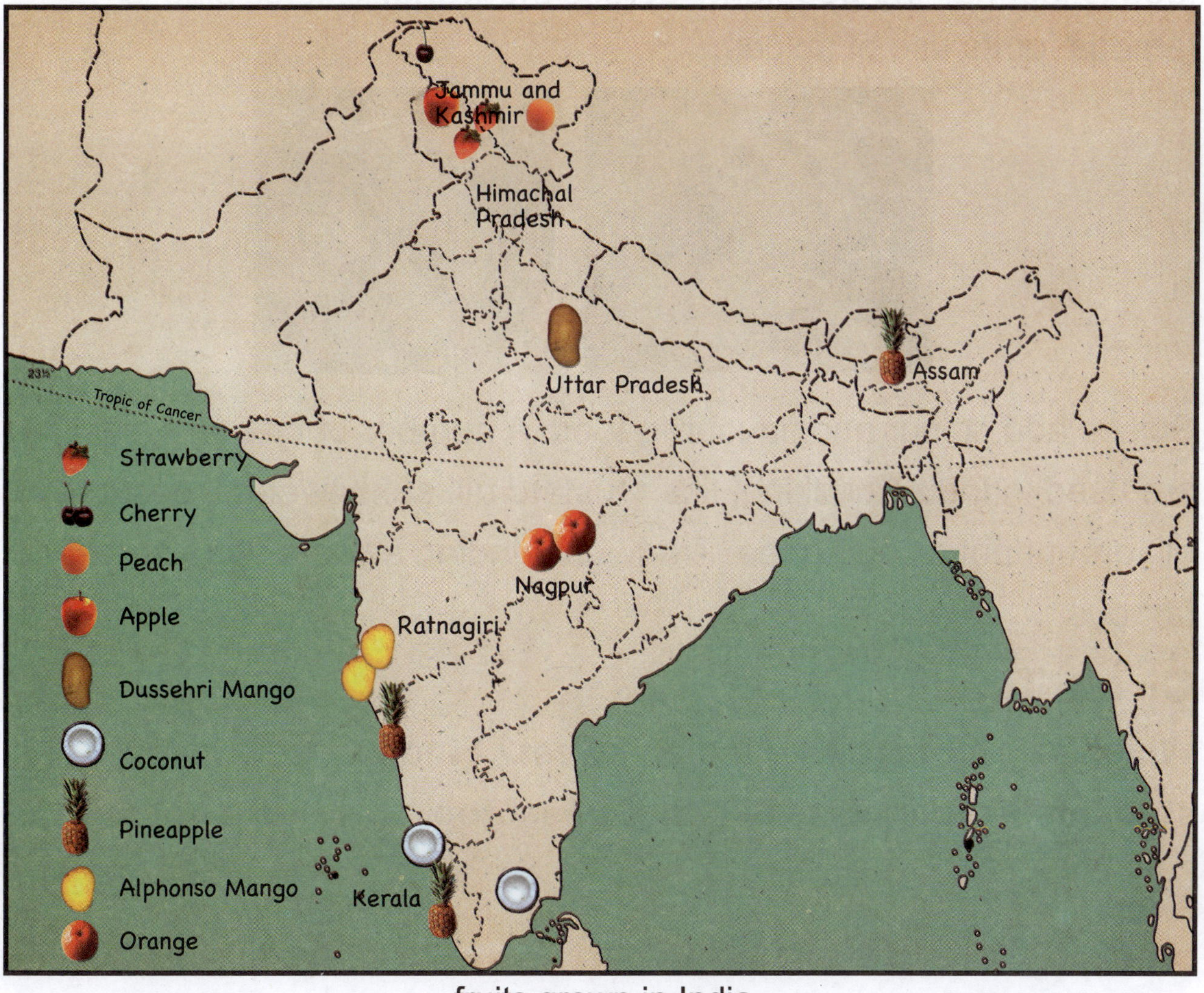

fruits grown in India

Coconuts grow abundantly in the warm coastal areas of Tamil Nadu and Kerala. Large harvests of pineapple come from Assam, Goa and Kerala. There are also several varieties of mangoes that are cultivated in India. Nagpur in Maharashtra is known as the Orange City because it is famous for its oranges. Himachal Pradesh and Ladakh produce a variety of apples. Jammu and Kashmir is also famous for its apples, as well as cherries and peaches.

Mango is the national fruit of India. Use the Internet or an encyclopedia to find out the national fruit of five other countries. Present your findings in class.

Food preparation varies across regions in India. However, Indian food is fast gaining popularity across the world. This cuisine is famous for its use of spices.

Spices add colour and flavour to food. A number of different oils are used in Indian cooking, like mustard oil, sunflower oil, sesame oil, groundnut oil and ghee. Traditional Indian sweets are also very famous.

Circle Time

Which is your favourite Indian sweet? Find out how many students in your class like that sweet too.

Clothing

People dress differently in different regions of the country. The clothes that people wear are influenced by the climate of that region. India experiences a large variety of climatic conditions. The northern regions of our country, such as Leh and Ladakh, experience cold weather for most parts of the year. People in cold regions wear woollen clothes, such as shawls, scarves and sweaters, to keep their bodies warm. On the other hand, the southern states, such as Andhra Pradesh, Telangana and Tamil Nadu, experience warm weather for most parts of the year. People in these warmer states of the south wear lighter cotton clothes for most parts of the year. Synthetic or nylon clothes are worn in the rainy season as they do not absorb water. People also use umbrellas and raincoats in the monsoon.

Factastic!

Mahatma Gandhi urged the people of India to wear **khadi** garments as a symbol of their Indian identity.

The most popular items of clothing among women in India are the *saree* and the *salwar kameez*, while most men in India wear *kurta-churidar* or shirts and trousers.

saree

salwar kameez

kurta churidar

kurta churidar

khadi: any cloth that is hand spun or hand woven

mundu
Kerala

dokhona
Assam

lungi shirt
South India

dhoti kurta
Bengal

Each state also has its own distinct traditional wear. Here are a few examples of the traditional wear of different Indian states.

Kerala (*mundu, saree*)

Gujarat (*kurta, turban, chaniya, choli, odhni*)

Kashmir (*pheran, turban, taranga*)

Nagaland (*mechala, shawl, ratapfe*)

Apart from traditional Indian clothes, men and women today also wear western clothes, such as dresses, trousers, skirts and jeans. People wear traditional clothes at weddings as well as on festivals and other special occasions.

Learn More

Dress up in the traditional clothes of your home state and say a few lines about your state in your mother tongue.

Self Check

- The food and clothes of Indians vary from state to state. ☐
- The food that people eat in a particular region is the staple food of that region. ☐
- A variety of spices are used in Indian food. ☐
- People wear traditional clothes on special occasions. ☐

____

____

Practice

1. Fill in the blanks with the correct words from the brackets.

a. In the northern parts of India, ____________ is preferred over rice. (wheat/pulses/fruits)

b. The ____________ is one of the most common pieces of clothing worn by Indian women. (*saree*/jeans/pyjamas)

c. ____________ grows best in regions with high rainfall. (Rice/Wheat/Fruits)

d. ____________ grows in areas with low rainfall. (*Bajra*/Sugarcane/Rice)

e. People living in Leh and Ladakh wear __________ clothes for most parts of the year. (cotton/woollen/nylon)

2. **Write T for true and F for false.**

a. We wear cotton clothes to keep us warm in winter. ☐

b. In the northern part of India, *bajra* is the staple food. ☐

c. Leh and Ladakh experience warm weather throughout the year. ☐

d. Gandhiji urged Indians to wear *khadi* garments. ☐

e. Nylon clothes do not get wet easily. ☐

3. **Answer the following questions.**

a. What is staple food?

b. Name five items of clothing that are worn by women in India.

c. What are spices? Name any five.

d. What type of clothes do people wear in the hilly areas in winter?

e. Is eating spices in food good for health?

f. Can we grow coconuts in Uttar Pradesh? Support your answer with proper reasoning.

4. **Critical Thinking**

a. Why do people in different parts of India eat different kinds of food?

b. People in the states of the south wear light cotton clothes. Why?

5. **Social Emotional Skills**

Should we make fun of or show disgust at someone else's food? Discuss.

6. **Creativity**

Collect pictures of various types of food eaten in different states of India and then work in a group to make a collage.

7 Indian Culture and Tradition

Explore

Which is your favourite Indian festival? What do you like the most about it?

Draw a picture of your family and friends celebrating this festival.

India is a land of diverse cultures and traditions. Festivals are a time for celebration. They are an integral part of our rich heritage and are celebrated for different reasons. They are celebrated to welcome the seasons of the year, to mark the different phases of the moon, to welcome the new year and to mark the birthdays of saints, gurus and leaders.

Although the same festivals may be celebrated in various parts of the country, they may be known by different names. In India, so many festivals are celebrated that not a single month goes by without a festival.

Holi

Known as the festival of colours, Holi marks the end of winter and the onset of summer. Children play with water balloons and *pichkaris*. People throw coloured powder and water on each other and eat sweets such as *gujjias* and *malpuas*. The traditional drink served on Holi is *thandai*.

Holi is also associated with the **Puranic story** of *Holika*, the sister of *Hiranyakashyap*, the demon-king. *Holika* had received a boon that she would remain safe even in a fire. Once, when the demon-king wanted to punish his son, *Prahlad*, who was a devotee of Lord Narayana,

Puranic story: story from the *puranas*, an important Hindu religious text

Prahlad was made to sit on *Holika's* lap in a pyre. When the **pyre** was lit, *Holika* was burned to ashes but *Prahlad* remained unharmed.

Factastic!

Holi is celebrated with fervor in Mathura and Vrindavan. **Raaslila** or the divine dance is performed by the devotees of Lord Krishna.

Basant Panchami

Basant Panchami marks the beginning of spring or *basant*. It is celebrated mainly in Punjab and Haryana, when the mustard crops are in full bloom and the fields look like they are covered with a thick yellow blanket. People dress in shades of yellow and apply a *tika* on their foreheads.

Saraswati Puja

Saraswati Puja is performed on Basant Panchami in some states. Students seek the blessings of Saraswati—the goddess of learning—on this day. It is a tradition to fly kites, wear yellow clothes and prepare sweet yellow (or saffron) rice on Basant Panchami.

Factastic!

Basant Panchami is celebrated on the fifth day of the Indian month of *Maagh* (January–February).

pyre: a large pile of wood for burning

Raksha Bandhan

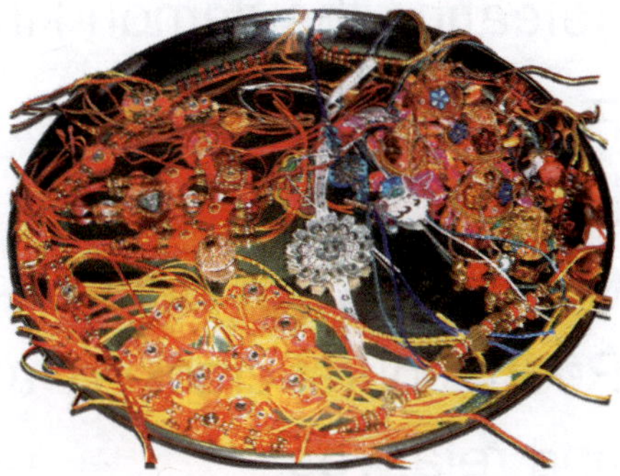

rakhi

Raksha Bandhan means 'a bond of protection'. It is a festival that celebrates the bond between brothers and sisters. On this day, sisters tie colourful *rakhis* around their brothers' wrists. Brothers also promise to protect their sisters from harm. Raksha Bandhan falls on *Shravan Purnima*, usually in the month of August.

Dussehra

Dussehra is also known as Vijayadashami. '*Vijay*' means victory and '*Dashmi*' means the tenth day. It marks the victory of good over evil, as it is believed that Lord Rama killed Ravana, the demon-king of Lanka, on this day. Ramlila is performed, enacting the battle between Lord Rama and Ravana. Effigies of Ravana, his brother Kumbhakarna and son Meghanad are burnt, symbolising the defeat of evil. In West Bengal, Dusshera marks the end of **Durga Puja**.

> **Factastic!**
>
> Navratri, the nine days preceding Vijayadashmi, are also celebrated in Gujarat. During Navratri, men and women perform the *garba* and *rasa* dances.

Diwali

Diwali is celebrated eighteen days after Dusshera. It is known as the festival of lights. Oil lamps (popularly known as *diyas*) are lit and are used to decorate homes.

In north India, Diwali marks Lord Rama's return to Ayodhya, after defeating the demon-king Ravana.

People clean and decorate their homes on Diwali. They wear new clothes. In the evening, prayers are offered to Goddess Lakshmi—the goddess of wealth—following which *diyas* and candles are lit. People burst crackers and exchange sweets with their friends and relatives.

Gurupurab

Gurupurab is celebrated by Sikhs thrice a year to mark the birthdays of Guru Nanak Dev, Guru Gobind Singh and Guru Tegh Bahadur. During the three days leading up to Gurupurab, the **Guru Granth Sahib** is read continuously in *gurudwaras*. This is known as the *Akhand Path*. On the day of the festival, the holy book is decorated. People visit *gurudwaras* to offer prayers and eat *langar*.

Find out what *Prabhat Pheris* are. Have you ever seen one?

Eid-ul-Fitr

Eid

Eid-ul-Fitr is celebrated by Muslims on the first day of **Shawwal**, marking the end of the holy month of Ramadan. During Ramadan, Muslims observe *roza*, a month-long fasting period. Eid, meaning festivity in Arabic, is celebrated after seeing the new crescent moon the previous evening. It is a time when Muslims give thanks for the blessings they have received from Allah. Families decorate their homes, gifts are given to friends and family, sweets and other delicacies are prepared, and new clothes are worn to celebrate the occasion.

Shawwal: the tenth month of the Islamic calendar, following the month of Ramadan

Christmas

Christmas

Christmas is celebrated on 25 December every year to celebrate the birth of Jesus Christ. People decorate Christmas trees in their homes and exchange gifts with their friends and family. Christians attend a special Christmas service at the church. This service is, however, open for all to attend.

Buddh Purnima

Buddh Purnima is celebrated to mark the birth of Lord Buddha. Buddh Purnima is celebrated on a full moon day in the month of April or May.

Mahavir Jayanti

Mahavir Jayanti is a festival of the Jains. The birth of Lord Mahavir is celebrated on this day.

Circle Time

Find information about the following festivals. Discuss.

Pongal ______________________________

____

Onam ______________________________

____

Basant Panchami ______________________________

____

Gudi Padwa ______________________________

____

Navroz ____

____

Baisakhi ____

____

Watch a video clip of the different classical dance forms of India. Observe the costumes which the dancers wear.

Dance

Indian dance and music originated as a means of offering thanks to deities as well as a means of worship.

The diversity of Indian culture is reflected in the range of dance forms. Every region has a dance form specific to it. There are two types of dances—**classical** and **folk**.

Kuchipudi from Andhra Pradesh

In the olden days, classical dances were only performed on special occasions and at special places, usually the temples. But nowadays, these dances are performed on stage as well.

The dancers train with gurus or teachers for several years. Classical dancers wear colourful costumes and jewellery and use a lot of make-up when performing their dances.

In folk dances, the dancers do not necessarily have to be trained. Most folk dances involve a lot of footwork, body and hand movements along with facial expressions. They are performed solo or in groups.

Some classical dance forms of India

Odissi from Odisha

Bharatnatyam from Tamil Nadu

Kathakali from Kerala

Some folk dances of India

Bhangra from Punjab

Angami dance from Nagaland

Cheraw or Bamboo dance from Mizoram

Jhumur dance from Assam

Ghoomar from Rajasthan

Folk dances are performed to celebrate a festival, the harvest season or to usher in a new season. They are usually accompanied by folk songs and musical instruments.

Learn More

Find out about other dance forms such as ballet, salsa and jazz. These are popular in the West.

Music

Indian music includes a wide variety of folk, popular and classical forms. Music is a very important part of our heritage and is associated with religious traditions and other celebrations. Classical music includes Carnatic music (in the south) and Hindustani music (in the north).

Community singing is also an important part of Indian culture. People sing *bhajans* in temples, the *gurbani* in *gurudwaras*, hymns in churches and *qawwalis* in *dargahs*.

> **Factastic!**
>
> Classical music originated in the *shlokas*, chanted by priests while performing religious ceremonies.

These are some of the musical instruments used in India.

tabla

sitar

dholak

veena

sarangi

santoor

Even though we may have different eating habits, wear different kinds of clothes and follow different religions, we are all proud to be part of one country—India and its cultural heritage.

Learn More

Learn a folk song and sing it in the class.

Self Check

- Festivals are an integral part of India's rich culture and traditions. ☐
- Some festivals are common to the whole country while some festivals are celebrated only in certain states. ☐
- Holi, Basant Panchami, Dussehra, Raksha Bandhan, Eid, Gurupurab and Christmas are common festivals we celebrate. ☐
- Every region in India has specific dances, both classical and folk. ☐
- India also has a wide variety of folk, popular and classical forms of music. ☐

Practice

1. The names of some Indian dances and musical instruments have been given in jumbled form below. Unscramble the words.

a. SSODII ______________________

b. RWCHEA ______________________

c. NAOOSTR ______________________

d. IIDUPCUHK ______________________

e. LABAT ______________________

f. RATIS ______________________

2. Write T for true and F for false.

a. The harvest festival of Tamil Nadu is called Onam. ☐

b. The dance form of Kuchipudi is native to Odisha. ☐

c. Navroz is celebrated on 25 December every year. ☐

d. Cheraw is a folk dance of Mizoram. ☐

e. Eid-ul-Fitr is celebrated in the month of Ramadan. ☐

3. Answer the following questions.

a. Write ten sentences about a festival you celebrate.

b. Name the holy book of the Sikhs. What is the *Akhand Path*?

c. How are folk dances different from classical dances?

d. When is Eid-ul-Fitr celebrated?

e. What would our lives be like if there were no festivals in India?

f. Do you think we should take certain safety measures while celebrating festivals?

4. **Critical Thinking**

a. Why do we celebrate different festivals?

b. Why is India called the land of festivals?

5. **Social Emotional Skills**

Not everyone can afford new clothes and sweets to celebrate festivals. How can you help them? Discuss.

6. **Creativity**

Make Diwali cards for your friends.

8 National Symbols and Emblems

Explore

Draw the logo or symbol of your school. What does it represent?

India is made up of a number of different states, each having its individual cultural identity. We are further diversified by our religions and customs. However, we still form one nation, India— and our national symbols and emblems give us our national identity.

National Symbols

National symbols are the living or non living things characterising a country. They are seen as emblems of it. The **Royal Bengal tiger** is our national animal. It symbolizes bravery and strength.

Royal Bengal tiger

Circle Time

The tiger is endangered in India because of poaching. Collect information about Project Tiger and tiger sanctuaries such as Ranthambore and the Sundarbans. Have a discussion in class on what students can do to help protect the tiger.

Our national bird is the **peacock**. It is famous for its beauty and unusual feathers. It symbolizes grace, pride and beauty.

peacock

The **lotus** is India's national flower. It is an aquatic plant that grows in shallow water. Despite growing in a muddy environment, it always appears clean and beautiful. The lotus flower symbolizes purity, wealth and knowledge.

lotus

Apart from India, the lotus is the national flower of another Asian country. Use the Internet or an encyclopedia to find out the name of this country.

The **banyan** tree is India's national tree. It is considered to be a sacred tree.

banyan tree

mango

The **mango** is India's national fruit. It has been cultivated in India since time immemorial.
There are over a hundred varieties of mangoes in India, in a range of colours, sizes and shapes. In India, we eat mangoes ripe, or prepare pickles and chutneys with unripe ones.

Our National Flag

The national flag is the symbol of the freedom and unity of our country. Our national flag is rectangular in shape and consists of three colours. It is, therefore, referred to as the tricolour

Indian national flag

or the *tiranga*. It has a deep saffron (*kesaria*) band at the top, a white band in the middle and a green band at the bottom. There is a navy blue wheel or *Dharma Chakra* in the middle of the white band. The saffron colour stands for strength and courage; the white stands for peace; and the green stands for growth and prosperity. The *Chakra* has twenty-four spokes representing the twenty four hours in a day. It symbolizes constant effort and growth.

The national flag can be hoisted at home, in school and in offices, keeping in mind these rules:

- The saffron band must always be at the top.
- No other flag can be placed above the tricolour.
- The flag must be taken down from the flag pole before sunset and folded carefully.
- We must always respect and honour our national flag.

Factastic!

The *Dharma Chakra*, also known as the *Ashoka Chakra*, depicts the wheel of law. It has been adapted from the Sarnath Lion Capital, which was built in the third century BCE during the reign of the Mauryan Emperor Ashoka.

Our National Anthem

Learn the national anthem and sing it together in class.

Our national anthem, *Jana Gana Mana*, was written by Rabindranath Tagore. The original poem is written in Bengali and has five stanzas, but only the first stanza is sung in Hindi as the national anthem.

The national anthem is played or sung on national holidays, public functions and at international events.

Factastic!

It takes about fifty-two seconds to sing our national anthem. The national anthem of Bangladesh is also a poem penned by Rabindranath Tagore.

Our national song is *Vande Mataram*. It was composed in Sanskrit by Bankim Chandra Chattopadhyay. It was inspired by the freedom struggle.

Our National Emblem

Our national emblem has been adapted from the Sarnath Lion Capital, built by Mauryan Emperor Ashoka in Uttar Pradesh. The original Sarnath Lion Capital has four lions, standing back to back, mounted on an elaborate stone base. The emblem shows only three lions (the fourth is hidden from view). The base shows an elephant, a galloping horse, a bull and a lion over a bell-shaped lotus.

the Sarnath Lion Capital

The words *Satyameva Jayate* from the **Mundaka Upanishad** are written in the **Devanagari** script below the stone base. *Satyameva Jayate* means 'Truth Alone Triumphs'.

Learn More

Which is the national sport of India? Discuss it in class.

Self Check

- National symbols are symbols which represent our country. ☐
- Our national flag has three colours. ☐

- Our national anthem is *Jana Gana Mana* and national song is *Vande Mataram*. ☐
- Our national emblem is adapted from the Sarnath Lion Capital. ☐

____

____

Practice

1. Fill in the blanks to complete the sentences.

a. Our national flag has a ____________ in the middle, which is ____________ in colour.

b. The national emblem is adapted from ____________.

c. The national animal of India is ____________.

d. *Jana Gana Mana* was written by ____________.

2. Match the following.

a. national anthem	i. peacock
b. national song	ii. tiger
c. national bird	iii. *Jana Gana Mana*
d. national flower	iv. *Vande Mataram*
e. national animal	v. lotus

3. Answer the following questions.

a. What is the *Dharma Chakra*?

b. Describe the Indian national flag.

c. What is the meaning of *Satyameva Jayate*?

d. When do we sing our national anthem?

e. Our national symbols make us feel united and proud. Explain.

f. We have different cultures and traditions in our country, but we are one nation. Discuss.

4. **Critical Thinking**

a. Why do we have national symbols?

b. Why is the national flag called the tricolour or *tiranga*?

5. **Social Emotional Skills**

We must always stand when the national anthem is being played. Do you agree with this and why?

6. **Creativity**

Find out and list the places/things where we see the national emblems. Draw/paste pictures.

9 Important Cities of India

Explore

Use an atlas to locate the following cities on a map of India.

1. New Delhi 2. Mumbai 3. Kolkata 4. Chennai

India is a vast country. Each state in India has many cities, big and small. Big cities with a population of more than one million are called metro cities. Mumbai, Chennai, Delhi, Kolkata, Hyderabad, Bengaluru, Pune and Ahmedabad are among the designated metro cities in India.

New Delhi

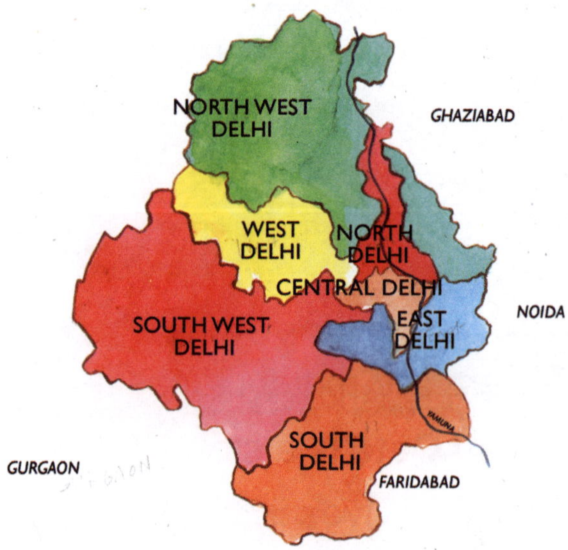

New Delhi is the capital of India. It is known as the National Capital Territory (NCT). It lies on the western bank of River Yamuna. It shares its borders with the states of Haryana and Uttar Pradesh.

The ancient city of Delhi is now referred to as Old Delhi. The newly-developed areas located towards its south now form New Delhi. The National Capital Region (NCR) of Delhi is an area comprising Old Delhi, New Delhi and a few towns spread over neighbouring states such as Rajasthan, Haryana and Uttar Pradesh. The prominent cities of NCR include Delhi, Ghaziabad, Faridabad, Gurugram, Noida and Meerut.

People and Government

New Delhi is a truly metropolitan city. People from all parts of India reside here. All central government offices are located in New Delhi.

The President, the Prime Minister and many important ministers and government officials also live here. The President of India lives in Rashtrapati Bhawan. Delhi has a **legislative assembly** and a chief minister. **Ambassadors** and high commissioners of various countries also reside in New Delhi.

Climate

Delhi experiences extreme climatic conditions. During the summer months, it is very hot. The summers stretch from April to October. Hot winds known as *loo* blow during the peak of summer, sometimes accompanied by dust storms as well. Monsoon is moderate while winters are very cold.

Industries

Delhi is a big commercial centre. Information technology, banking, manufacturing, leather processing and pharmaceuticals are some of the major industries of this region.

Tourist Attractions

There are many places in Delhi which are popular with tourists.

India Gate is a stone memorial built in the memory of soldiers who lost their lives in World War I.

Rajpath is an important road in central Delhi. This is where the Republic Day parade is held.

Rashtrapati Bhawan, the official residence of the President of India, is situated on Raisina Hill.

Red Fort, also known as Lal Quila, was built by the Mughal Emperor Shah Jahan.

Raj Ghat is a memorial dedicated to Mahatma Gandhi.

Jama Masjid is the largest mosque in India.

legislative assembly: a group having legislative or law-making powers
ambassadors: diplomats sent by countries as their representatives to foreign countries

Qutab Minar, which was constructed by Qutab-ud-din Aibak, is the world's tallest brick minaret.

India Gate

Qutab Minar

Red Fort

Jama Masjid

Other places of interest in Delhi include the **Bahai Lotus Temple**, **Jantar Mantar**, **Lodi Garden**, **Iskcon temple**, **Akshardham Temple**, **Humayun's Tomb**, **Nehru Planetarium**, **Gurudwara Bangla Sahib**, **St. James Church** and **Chandni Chowk**, which is a very busy market located opposite the Red Fort.

> **Factastic!**
>
> The Indira Gandhi International Airport in Delhi is the busiest airport in India. With the commencement of operations at the new Terminal 3, it has become South Asia's largest aviation hub.

Collect information about Delhi's metro transit system.

Mumbai

Find out any two things for which Mumbai is famous.

Mumbai, the capital of Maharashtra, is situated on the west coast of India by the Arabian Sea. Mumbai was earlier known as Bombay. The name of the city was officially changed in 1995. Mumbai is one of the most populated cities in the world. It is the commercial and entertainment hub of India. It is also considered to be India's economic capital.

The Governor, Chief Minister and cabinet ministers of Maharashtra reside in Mumbai.

Mumbai consists of two distinct areas: the town and the suburbs. The town region is commonly known as the Island City.

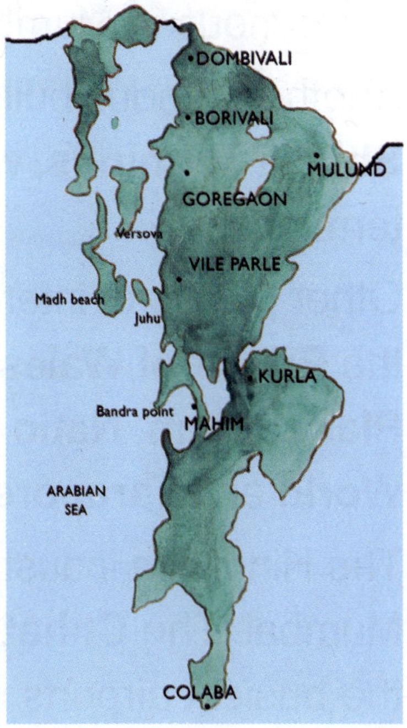

Climate

Since Mumbai is located next to the sea, it has warm, humid summers and pleasant winters. Between March and October, humidity is very high and the temperature ranges between 30°C and 35°C. During the monsoons, in June, July and August, it receives heavy rainfall.

Industries and Institutions

Mumbai has many factories that make textiles, medicines, oils, chemicals and electronic goods. India's most important petroleum field is situated at Bombay High, off the Mumbai coast. Being the largest port of India, Mumbai plays an important role in the import-export industry as well.

Other important institutions in Mumbai are the Bhabha Atomic Research Centre (BARC), the Tata Institute of Fundamental Research (TIFR) and the Indian Institute of Technology (IIT).

Tourist Attractions

There are many places in Mumbai which are popular with tourists.

The **Gateway of India** is one of the main tourist attractions of the city.

Marine Drive, also known as the Queen's Necklace, looks splendid when illuminated at night.

Juhu and **Girgaum Chowpatty** are two of the many beaches that are famous in Mumbai.

Gateway of India

Another famous building is the **Chhatrapati Shivaji Terminus**, which is a railway terminus.

Other places of interest in Mumbai are the **Prince of Wales Museum**, **Nehru Planetarium**, **National Science Centre**, **Hanging Gardens, Essel World** and **Taraporevala Aquarium.**

The Hindi film industry, **Bollywood**, is another very important part of Mumbai. The **Chhatrapati Shivaji International Airport** is one of the busiest airports in India.

The **Rajiv Gandhi Sea Link**, a cable-stayed bridge over the Arabian Sea, was inaugurated in 2009. It links Bandra to Worli.

Mumbai is famous for its *bhel puri*, *pav bhaji*, *vada-pav* and *srikhand*.

Marathi is the local language of Mumbaikers.

Find out which festivals are celebrated in Mumbai.

Kolkata

Where is Eden Gardens? Why is it famous?

Kolkata is the capital of West Bengal. It was known as Calcutta earlier and was officially renamed Kolkata in 2001. The city is situated on the banks of the River Hugli and faces the Bay of Bengal. Kolkata was once a fishing village, which has now grown to become one of India's most populated cities.

The offices of the West Bengal government are located in Kolkata. The Governor, the Chief Minister, other ministers and government officials live in the city.

Kolkata has a very rich and diverse culture. People are fond of dancing, singing, poetry and painting. The most popular games in Kolkata are football and cricket.

Climate

Like Mumbai, Kolkata also experiences warm and humid summers. As it lies in the eastern part of India, it receives heavy rainfall during the monsoon season. The winters are cool.

Industries and Institutions

Diamond Harbour is an important port in Kolkata. The main railway station is called Howrah Station. Kolkata's airport is called the Netaji Subhash Chandra Bose International Airport.

Rice, rubber, jute, textile, chemicals and paper are some of the important industries in Kolkata.

Tourist Attractions

Kolkata attracts many tourists every year. Some of the places popular with tourists are:

Victoria Memorial

- Fort William
- The Victoria Memorial (currently a museum famous for its statues and paintings)
- The Botanical Garden (known for its ancient banyan tree)
- The Indian Museum
- Alipore Zoo
- Birla Planetarium
- Ramakrishna Mission at Belur Math

- Eden Gardens
- The National Library (the biggest library in India)
- St. Paul's Cathedral

The staple diet of Bengalis is rice and fish. Kolkata is famous for sweets like *sandesh*, *rasogulla* and *mishti doi*. The people of Kolkata mainly speak Bengali.

Find out about the main festivals celebrated in Kolkata.

> **Factastic!**
>
> The old cantilever bridge on the River Hugli, known as the Rabindra Setu, connects Kolkata and Howrah. It is popularly known as the Howrah Bridge.

Chennai

What is Kollywood? Find out.

Chennai is the capital of Tamil Nadu.

It was formerly known as Madras. It was renamed in 1996. It is the fourth-largest metropolitan city in India. Located on the Coromandel Coast of the Bay of Bengal, it has attracted many traders and merchants.

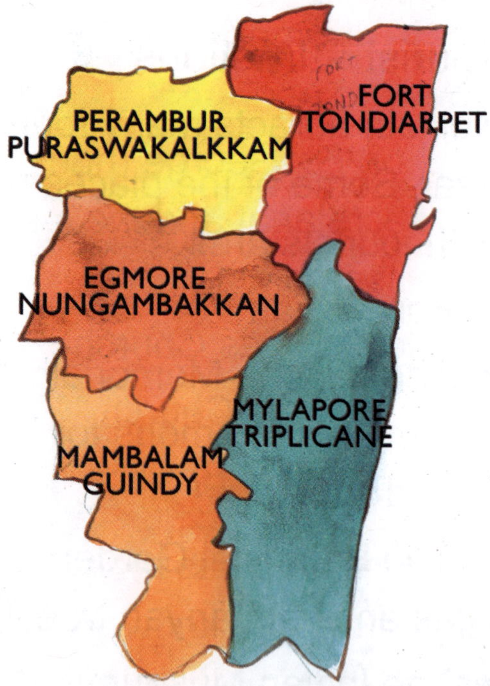

Chennai is the cultural capital of India.
It is known for its classical dance shows and Hindu temples.
The people of Chennai are fond of music and dance, and every year,

a music festival is organized where traditional Carnatic music artists perform. Chennai is also known for Bharatnatyam, a classical dance form that originated in Tamil Nadu.

The Governor of Tamil Nadu, the Chief Minister of the state and other ministers and government officials live in the city.

Climate

For most of the year, the weather in Chennai is hot and humid. The city gets most of its seasonal rainfall from mid-September to mid-December. Cyclones in the Bay of Bengal sometimes hit the city.

Industries

Chennai's economy is based on the automobile, technology, hardware manufacturing and healthcare industries.

Tourist Attractions

There are many places in Chennai that are popular with tourists. They are:

- Fort St. George (houses the secretariat and the legislative assembly)
- St. Thomas Church
- St. Mary's Church
- Santhome Basilica

Santhome Basilica

Chennai also has many beautiful Hindu temples known for their architecture and ***gopurams***.

Chennai's famous Snake Park is located inside Guindy National Park. It is popular with both locals and tourists.

Tamil and English are the two languages that are widely spoken in Chennai. The local dishes are *sambar*, *rasam*, *upma*, *vada*, *idli* and *dosa*.

Learn More

Find out the names of some popular Carnatic music singers and Bharatnatyam dancers.

Factastic!

The Marina Beach in Chennai stretches out over a distance of about 12 km.

Self Check

- Cities with a population of more than one million are called metro cities. ☐
- Delhi, Mumbai, Kolkata and Chennai are old and famous metro cities of India. ☐
- New Delhi is the capital of India. All central government offices are located here. ☐
- Delhi has extreme climatic conditions.
- There are many popular places in Delhi, like India Gate, Qutab Minar, Jama Masjid and Red Fort. ☐
- Mumbai is the commercial capital of India. The climate in Mumbai is moderate. It is warm and humid in summer and has pleasant winters. ☐
- Many popular places like the Gateway of India, Bhabha Atomic Research Centre, Chhatrapati Shivaji International Airport and Bollywood are part of Mumbai. ☐

- Kolkata is the capital of West Bengal and is famous for its rich and diverse culture. ☐
- The Victoria Memorial, Eden Gardens, Howrah Bridge and Birla Planetarium are famous tourist attractions in Kolkata. ☐
- Chennai is the capital of Tamil Nadu and the cultural capital of India. ☐
- It is known for its classical dance, music and Hindu temples. ☐

____

____

Practice

1. Draw lines to match the following.

a. film industry •	• sweet
b. *sandesh* •	• classical dance
c. Bharatnatyam •	• beach
d. Marina •	• Bollywood

2. Write T for true and F for false.

a. The people of Chennai speak only in Hindi. ☐

b. Mumbai is the commercial capital of India. ☐

c. The climate of Delhi is moderate. ☐

d. The staple diet of Bengalis is rice and fish. ☐

e. The Gateway of India is in Chennai. ☐

3. Answer the following questions.

a. What is NCR?

b. How is the climate of Delhi different from that of Mumbai?

c. List four tourist attractions of Kolkata.

d. Name the important industries in Chennai.

e. The Indira Gandhi International Airport is the busiest airport in India. Explain.

f. Seafood is very popular in cities like Kolkata and Mumbai. Discuss.

4. Critical Thinking

a. Why is rice the staple diet of Bengalis?

b. Why is Marine Drive known as the Queen's Necklace?

5. Social Emotional Skills

How are the lives of people living in metro cities different from those of the people living in villages?

6. Creativity

Make a project on the city of Bengaluru. Find out details about the city's history, its climate, the important industries, its major landmarks, its culture and its cuisine.

You can make your project in the form of a booklet, a chart or a computer display.

Part II

Science

10 Living and Non-living Things

Explore

Read the following sentences. Underline the living things in green and the non-living things in red.

a. The boy was playing with the dog.

b. Paper can be made from plants and trees.

c. Wood is used to make pencils.

d. Four people can play a game of carrom.

e. The cat sat on a tuft of grass under a tree.

We see plants, animals, the Sun, the Moon, chairs, tables, books, stones and many other things around us. Some of these are living and some are non-living. Some non-living things are naturally occurring and some are made by man.

Let us see the differences between living and non-living things.

Living things	Non-living things
Living things **breathe**. Living things breathe in oxygen to survive. Animals use lungs, fish use gills and plants use pores to breathe. 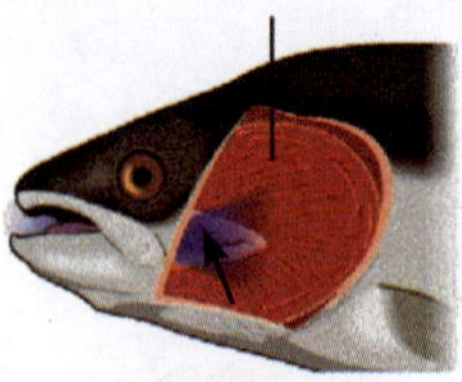 gills	Non-living things do not require oxygen and hence **do not breathe**.

Living things **can move** by themselves. Birds, animals and humans can run, jump, fly or swim.   A sunflower moves and turns to face the sunlight. A lotus flower opens its petals at sunrise and closes at sunset.	Non-living things **cannot move** by themselves. They need an outside force to move them. 
Living things **need food**, **water** and **sunlight** to survive. Food provides them with the energy to perform various activities and is required for their growth and development. Plants prepare their own food with the help of water, air and sunlight.	Non-living things **do not need food**, **water** or **sunlight.**
Living things **grow**. They undergo various changes during their growth.	Non-living things **do not grow** naturally.
Living things need to **remove waste** from their bodies. This process is called excretion.	Non-living things **do not need to remove** waste from their bodies.
Living things **react to changes in their environment**, such as heat, pressure or touch. We feel hot in summer, a pin prick hurts us and some flowers bloom with the warmth of the Sun.	Non-living things cannot sense **changes in their environment**.

 Living things **reproduce**. They produce more of their own kind. Trees produce seeds from which new plants and trees grow. A dog gives birth to puppies. Human beings produce babies.	Non-living things **do not reproduce**. 

Habitat

The natural environment of a living thing is known as its habitat. Some habitats are large, such as forests, seas and oceans. Others are quite small, such as our own backyard or the neighbourhood park. All living beings interact with their environment and with each other.

Factastic!

The leaves of the touch-me-not plant curl up if you touch them.

Learn More

Non-living things can be natural or man-made. List any ten man-made things present in your class.

Self Check

- We see living and non-living things around us. ☐
- Non-living things can be natural or man-made. ☐
- Living things breathe, need food, can move, show growth, react to changes and reproduce. Non-living things do not show these characteristics. ☐

- The natural environment of a living thing is called its habitat. ☐

____

____

Practice

1. Classify the things in the box below into living, man-made and natural non-living things.

sparrow	pants	tomato	plant	rocks	river	air
kangaroo	frog	paper	factory	pen	chair	Sun

Living	Man-made	Natural non-living

2. Write T for true and F for false. Correct the false statements.

a. Plants move from one place to another in search of food and shelter.

b. Non-living things are either produced by humans or are naturally present.

c. Food gives us energy to move and work.

d. Living things do not react to changes in their environment.

e. The Sun, the Moon and the stars are natural non-living things.

3. **Answer the following questions.**

a. List three differences between living and non-living things.

b. Define habitat. Give examples.

c. Name some breathing organs of living things.

d. Arnav made the following observations about a plant and a worm. Which of these are correct?

(i) A plant cannot reproduce, a worm can.

(ii) A plant does not need food, while the worm makes its own food.

(iii) A worm can go anywhere but the plant cannot.

(iv) Both do not respond to stimuli.

e. Rina touched the leaves of a mimosa plant and they closed. This shows that

(i) it can grow.

(ii) it responds to stimuli.

(iii) it can reproduce.

(iv) it can move from place to place.

f. What would happen if all living things stopped reproducing?

4. **Critical Thinking**

a. Why do human beings need food?

b. Why do animals move from one place to another?

5. **Social Emotional Skills**

Do non-living things also need care?

6. **Creativity**

Living things reproduce and have young ones. Collect pictures of animals and their offspring from magazines or the Internet. Create a chart and display it in class.

11 Parts of a Plant

Explore

Go for a nature walk. Uproot one plant for the entire class. Take turns to observe the plant and list all the parts you see.

____

____

Plants can grow in the plains, in deserts, on mountains and in water. They exist in different shapes, sizes and colours. It is important for us to understand the basic structure of a plant and its functions.

A plant can be divided into two main parts—the part that grows below the ground, known as the **root** and the part that grows above the ground, known as the **shoot**. The shoot consists of **stems**, **leaves**, **flowers** and **fruits**.

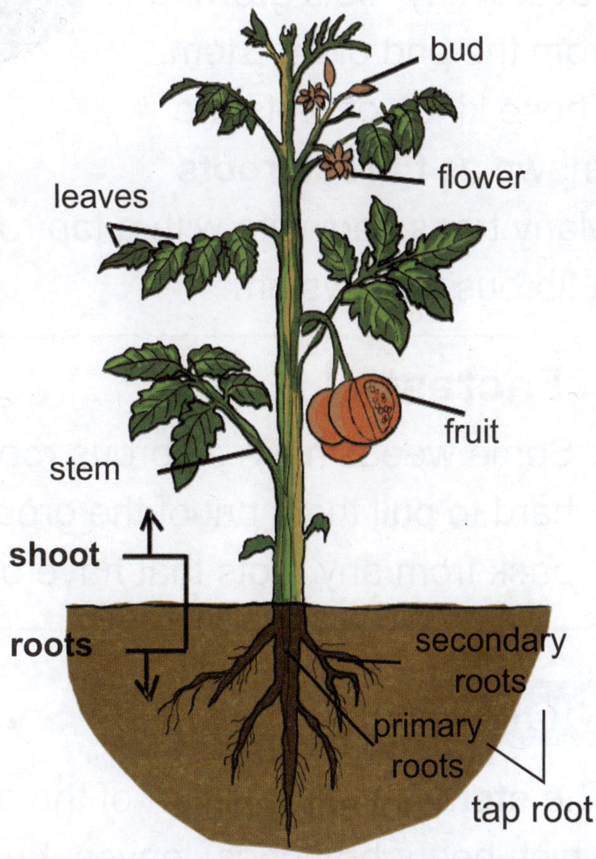

Roots

The **root** anchors the plant to the soil and absorbs water and minerals. There are two main types of roots—**tap root** and **fibrous root**.

Tap Root

Some plants, such as mango, radish and carrot, have one main root growing straight downwards from the stem into the soil. This main root is called the primary root. Smaller roots, known as lateral roots, grow from the primary root. This kind of a root is called a **tap root**.

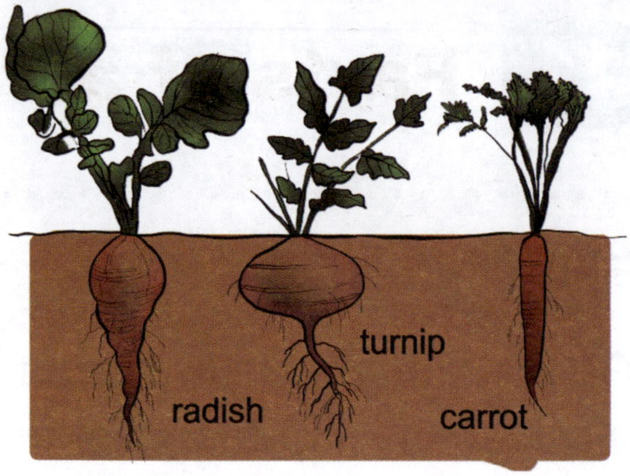

plants having tap root

Fibrous Root

Plants such as grass, coconut and onion have several tiny roots growing from the end of the stem. These kinds of roots are known as **fibrous roots**.

grass

onion

Many trees begin life with a tap root, but after a few years change to a fibrous root system.

> **Factastic!**
>
> Some weeds have a fibrous root system. This makes it very hard to pull them out of the ground. Pulled-out weeds can grow back from any roots that have been left behind in the soil.

Stem

The **stem** is the main part of the shoot which bears branches, leaves, buds and flowers.

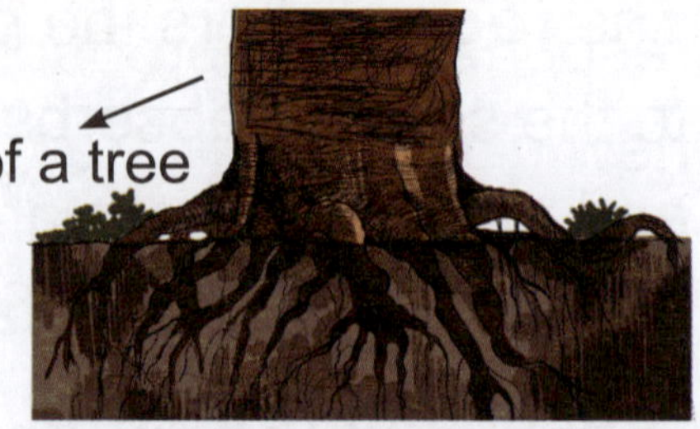
stem of a tree

lateral: extension, as a branch or shoot

stem of a climber

The stem transports water and nutrients from the roots to all parts of the plant and supports the weight of the plant. It also carries food made by the leaves to the other parts of the plant. Some plants have strong stems, like trees. Others have weak stems, like herbs and climbers.

Leaves

Leaves grow on stems. They are responsible for converting sunlight into food. Plants manufacture food using carbon dioxide and water, in the presence of sunlight and a green-coloured pigment called chlorophyll, which is found in all green plants. This process of making food by green plants is known as photosynthesis. (Photo meaning light and synthesis meaning mixing together). Oxygen is released during this process. Food is stored in different parts of the plant in the form of starch or sugar.

Flowers

rose flower

Flowers also grow on stems. They can be of different shapes and colours. Flowers are structures responsible for producing seeds. Seeds grow into new plants. Thus, flowers help a plant grow more of its own kind. Some flowers change into **fruits**. Most fruits also have seeds inside them.

Seeds

Seeds can be of different shapes, sizes and colours. A seed grows into a plant. We can eat certain seeds and these are known as edible seeds. Examples are wheat, rice, beans, pulses, sunflower and pumpkin. Some seeds are, however, inedible and we do not consume them.

wheat rice beans corn

Name two edible and two inedible seeds.

edible: ____________________ ____________________

inedible: ____________________ ____________________

Seeds germinate into plants in the presence of sunlight, water, right temperature conditions and in a safe place. Some seeds may lie dormant for a few years until the right conditions arise.

Factastic!

Plants adapt in different ways to survive. An indoor plant near a window bends towards the light. Many plants in shady areas grow larger leaves so that they may receive more sunlight. Plants that grow in dry places grow longer roots to find water deep underground.

Circle Time

Plants are all around us. Discuss with your friends the uses and importance of plants and the ways to protect and conserve them.

dormant: lying asleep or as if asleep; inactive
conserve: to use or manage (natural resources) wisely; preserve; save

Learn More

Where do the following plants store food? Circle the correct answer.

coconut	leaf	stem	fruit	seed	root
carrot	leaf	stem	fruit	seed	root
spinach	leaf	stem	fruit	seed	root
cucumber	leaf	stem	fruit	seed	root
tomato	leaf	stem	fruit	seed	root
cabbage	leaf	stem	fruit	seed	root
rajma	leaf	stem	fruit	seed	root

Self Check

- Plants have two main parts, the root and the shoot. ☐
- The root grows below the ground and the shoot grows above the ground. ☐
- Roots provide support, water and minerals to the plant. ☐
- The stem bears leaves, buds and flowers. ☐
- The stem also transports water and nutrients to different parts of the plant and provides support. ☐
- Green leaves prepare food for the plant. ☐
- Fruits have one or more seeds and seeds grow into new plants. ☐

____

____

Practice

1. Complete the crossword.

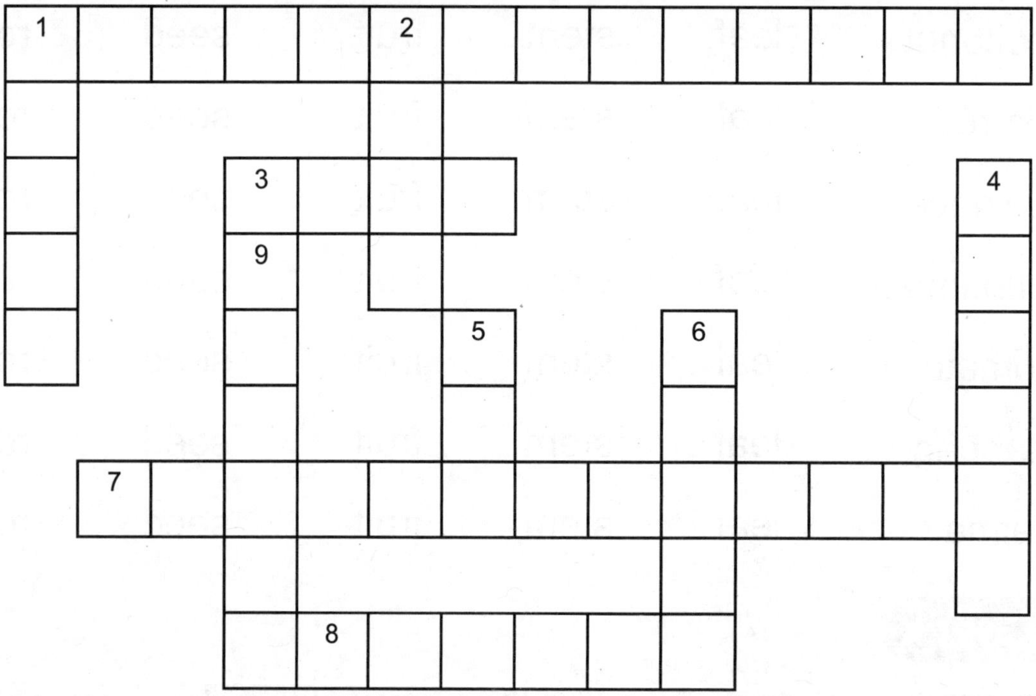

ACROSS

1 Plants make their food through this process

3 It bears leaves, flowers and fruits

7 Plants need this gas for photosynthesis

8 The part where most plants make their food

DOWN

1 Unscramble NLPAT

2 It germinates to form a plant

4 Plants produce and release this gas

5 Source of energy and warmth

6 Used by many plants to absorb water and minerals from the soil

9 Food is stored in the different parts of a plant in the form of

2. **Write O for the fruits that have one seed and M for the fruits that have many seeds.**

orange

mango

water melon

papaya

apple

peach

3. **Answer the following questions.**

   a. Define photosynthesis.

   b. Give four examples of leaves that we eat.

   c. What is chlorophyll?

   d. Which of the following is not a root?

      (i) Carrot   (ii) Potato

      (iii) Radish   (iv) Beetroot

   e. Grapevines are an example of a climber. They climb because

      (i) they have weak stems and need support

      (ii) they love to climb

      (iii) they can only bear fruit at a certain height

      (iv) none of the above

   f. What would happen if there were no flowers?

4. **Critical Thinking**

a. Why is the flower an important part of a plant?

b. The leaf is known as the kitchen of the plant. Why?

5. **Social Emotional Skills**

How are plants and animals dependent on each other? Discuss.

6. **Creativity**

Collect different types of pulses and leaves.
Work in groups and make collages.

12 Animals

Explore

Guess the names of the following animals.

a. I can live both in water and on land, and I croak. __________

b. I love bananas and live on trees. __________

c. I weave webs to trap insects and eat them. _____

d. I am slow, but I can live more than a hundred years. _____

e. I have a long neck, and I eat the leaves of tall trees. _________

Animals live all around us. They live in the sea, in trees, on land and sometimes deep under the ground. Tiny insects to enormous whales are all part of the animal kingdom. With such a variety of animals in the world, it is essential to classify them into groups.

Different animals eat different types of food. Their special feeding organs help them eat the food of their choice. Animals can be put into different groups based on the food they eat.

Animals

Herbivores | Carnivores | Omnivores | Frugivores

Herbivores are animals that eat only plants. Cows, giraffes, deer and goats are examples of herbivorous animals. Their sharp front teeth help them tear off leaves from plants. Strong, broad teeth at the back of their mouth help them chew their food.

Some animals such as lions and tigers only eat the flesh of other animals. These animals are called **carnivores**. They have sharp, pointed and curved teeth for tearing flesh.

Omnivores are animals that eat plants as well as the flesh of other animals. Crows, bears and humans are examples of omnivores. They have strong grinding teeth for chewing flesh and bones.

Animals that mostly eat fruits are called **frugivores**. Some of these animals use their teeth, while others use their beaks. Bats and parrots are examples of frugivores.

Food Chain

All animals are directly or indirectly dependent on plants for food. Only green plants can prepare their own food by photosynthesis. All green plants are called producers as they prepare food for other animals and plants. All other living beings obtain food from plants, therefore they are called consumers. Herbivores eat plants directly. All carnivores eat herbivores. This chain of living beings eating and being eaten is called the food chain. For example, a deer eats plants and a lion eats the deer. All the food chains always start with plants.

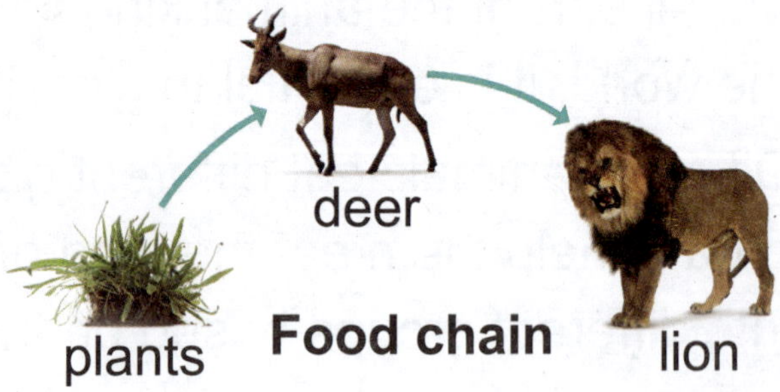

Food chain

Growth and Reproduction

All living things grow. Babies grow into adults and adults grow old and eventually die.

growth in humans

Living beings reproduce and give birth to young ones, and this cycle is repeated. All animals reproduce by

- giving birth to young ones.
- laying eggs.

Animals such as dogs, cats, deer, lions and elephants give birth to young ones and take care of them.

Animals such as fish, snakes, frogs, crocodiles and birds lay eggs.

Based on where they live, how they look and how they give birth to their young, animals are classified into different groups.

life cycle of a hen

Animals

- Fish
- Amphibians
- Reptiles
- Birds
- Mammals
- Insects

Fish can breathe under water. They breathe with the help of gills. They live and lay their eggs in water. Most fish are covered with small, smooth plates called scales.

barracuda

blue fish

clown fish

Amphibians can live on land and in water. They lay squishy eggs in water where their young ones hatch and grow. They need to keep their bodies moist to stay alive so they have soft, damp skin; for example, frogs and toads. A young frog breathes underwater with gills, whereas an adult frog develops lungs and can breathe on land.

mudskipper

green frog

toad

Reptiles have dry, scaly skin. Most reptiles lay eggs to produce young ones. Reptiles are cold-blooded, that is, their body temperature changes according to their surroundings. Reptiles breathe with the help of lungs.

chameleon

water monitor

crocodiles

Birds are the only animals with feathers. Though all birds have wings, not all can fly; for example, penguins. All birds lay eggs and take care of their babies. They breathe with the help of lungs.

snowbird

sarus crane

kingfisher

Mammals are warm-blooded animals. These animals can keep their body temperature higher than their surroundings. They give birth to young ones and feed their babies milk. They breathe with the help of lungs. Most mammals have hair or fur covering their bodies.

tiger

langur

hippopotamus

Insects are small creatures, for example, spiders, centipedes and butterflies. Most insects have six legs and can fly. Insects breathe with the help of small holes called spiracles. There are approximately two million different types of insects in the world.

butterfly

grasshopper

housefly

ant

Factastic!

Insects and fish have no eyelids. Hardened lenses protect their eyes.

Learn More

Never make a camel angry, for it will spit at you. Find out other such fun facts about animals and share them with the rest of the class.

Self Check

- On the basis of the food they eat, animals are grouped into herbivores, carnivores, omnivores and frugivores. ☐
- All animals grow and reproduce. ☐
- Animals reproduce by laying eggs or by giving birth to young ones. ☐
- Animals are grouped on the basis of their body structure and habits. ☐
- Fish live in water and lay eggs. ☐
- Amphibians can live on land as well as in water. ☐
- Reptiles have dry, scaly skin and are cold-blooded animals. ☐
- Birds have feathers and can fly. ☐
- Mammals are warm-blooded animals. They give birth to young ones and feed their babies milk. ☐
- Insects mostly have six legs and wings to fly. ☐

____

____

Practice

1. Name three animals that

a. live on land ____________ ____________ ____________

b. live in water ____________ ____________ ____________

c. can fly ____________ ____________ ____________

d. can swim ____________ ____________ ____________

e. can hop ____________ ____________ ____________

2. Classify these animals as amphibian, fish, reptile, bird or mammal.

parrot	turtle	snake	dolphin	swan
shark	gorilla	salamander	leopard	seal
bat	peacock	elephant	lion	chimpanzee

amphibian	fish	reptile	bird	mammal

3. Answer the following questions.

a. What are mammals? How are they different from insects?

b. Differentiate between herbivores and carnivores.

c. What is food chain? Explain with the help of an example.

d. Pick the odd one out.

(i) Elephant (ii) Lion

(iii) Hyena (iv) Jackal

e. A food chain always starts with

(i) animals (ii) insects

(iii) green plants (iv) birds

f. What will happen if all tigers are killed?

4. Critical Thinking

a. Why are humans called omnivores?

b. Why are plants called producers?

5. Social Emotional Skills

Do you use articles made from animal skins? Many animals are killed for their skin. Is it right to kill animals for commercial purposes? Discuss.

6. Creativity

Go for a nature walk around your school or home. Find one example of the following kinds of animals. Name them, draw/paste their pictures and make a chart.

Two-legged Four-legged

Six-legged Eight-legged

Many-legged

13 Birds

Explore

Go for a nature walk. Observe different types of birds, shape of their beaks, their claws and their movements. Draw the beaks of any five birds.

Birds are beautiful, coloured living beings. They usually have a beak, two wings and two legs. Their beaks and claws help them to catch prey and build nests. Most birds can fly.

- Birds fly with the help of wings. They flap their wings upwards and downwards to fly.
- Strong flight muscles help them to move their wings.
- They have hollow bones which make their bodies light.
- They have streamlined bodies.
- Their tails help them to change direction.

Feathers

A bird's body and its wings are covered with small, fluffy feathers.

There are three types of feathers:

- **Down feathers** are found all over the body of the bird and help it to stay warm.
- **Flight feathers** are long and flat and are found on the wings and the tail. These help the bird to steer and fly.
- **Body** or **contour feathers** give shape and colour to the bird. With the exception of the beak, legs and feet, a bird is completely covered with body feathers.

streamlined: narrow at front and broad in the middle

Most birds use their feathers and wings to fly, but birds such as penguins, that cannot fly, use their wings to swim in water.

Beaks

A bird uses its beak to catch food and eat. Different birds have different kinds of beaks, depending upon the type of food they eat. Some birds, such as toucans, have very colourful beaks.

robin

Birds such as robins, sparrows and pigeons have beaks like a nutcracker, which are perfect for breaking open seeds. These birds have strong, short, thick and cone-shaped beaks.

Flesh-eating birds, such as eagles, vultures and hawks, have strong, sharp and hooked beaks that help them tear flesh. They eat other smaller-sized birds, as well as animals such as rabbits and lambs.

eagle

hummingbird

Some birds, such as the hummingbird and the sunbird, have beaks like straws. Their long, pointed beaks help them to drink nectar from flowers. The beak acts like a straw and helps it to reach deep into flowers and sip nectar.

hoopoe

The woodpecker and the hoopoe have strong chisel-shaped beaks which help them to poke holes into hard tree trunks and pull out insects.

Some water birds, such as ducks, geese and some types of cranes, have broad and flat beaks, known as **bills**, with holes on either side. These birds take in muddy water containing insects, worms and plants.

spoonbill

The beak acts as a strainer, as the muddy water flows out through the holes, leaving behind the worms and the small fish in the bird's bill.

The great blue heron uses its sharp beak to look for food at the water's edge. The beak is used as a spear to grab fish, snakes and frogs.

blue heron

Claws

Read the clues and match the correct feet to each bird.

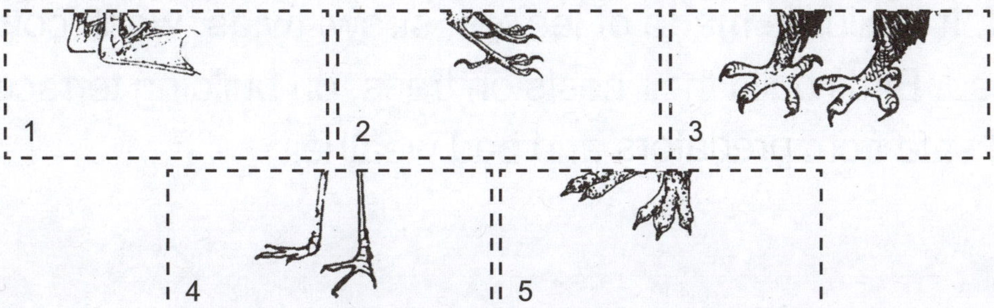

Birds have two feet. Each foot usually has four toes, three facing forward and one rearward. Birds use their feet to walk, to hop around and to hold their food and branches of trees. Peacocks and hens have sharp claws to dig the ground for food.

hen

eagle

Eagles and vultures have very sharp claws, known as talons. These help them to catch their prey, such as frogs, mice and rats.

woodpecker

Woodpeckers have two toes pointing in the upward direction and the other two in the downward direction. This helps them to climb trees.

Crows, sparrows, pigeons and parrots use their feet to hold the branches of trees as they perch on them.

duck

Ducks and geese have webbed feet that help them swim in water. The webbing helps them to paddle and push water. Herons and cranes have long legs with the toes spread out, which helps them wade through water.

Nests

Birds also have homes. A bird's home is known as a nest. Birds make their nests only when they have to lay eggs, so as to keep their eggs protected. It could be made of leaves, straw, twigs, wool, cotton or even thread. Birds build their nests on trees, on building terraces and in any place safe from predators and bad weather.

perch: to sit on something high; place where a bird sits
wade: to walk through water
predator: an animal that hunts, kills and eats other animals

tailor bird

Tailor birds make their nest by sewing together leaves with their needle shaped beaks.

weaver bird

The weaver bird weaves pieces of leaves, grass or twigs together to build a nest. The nest has a tunnel-like opening at the bottom for the bird to enter.

woodpecker

The woodpecker uses its beak to peck at tree trunks and make a hole in the tree. It makes a nest inside this hole.

penguin

Since it is difficult to find straw, twigs and grass in cold regions, penguins make nests out of pebbles.

Factastic!

The female cuckoo bird looks for a nest of another bird, which already has eggs in it. She pushes the eggs out and lays her own. When the baby cuckoo is born, the foster parents continue to work hard to feed it, even though the baby cuckoo bird may grow to be many times bigger than them.

Migration

In extremely cold conditions, birds move to warm places. They fly long distances and move to places with plenty of food, water and better weather conditions. This mass movement of birds is called migration. Birds migrate every year in the same season.

Learn More

Use the colour key to colour the picture of the scarlet macaw. Use the encyclopedia to find out more about it.

2 – bright blue
4 – black
5 – brown
6 – red
7 – yellow
9 – purple
10 – white

Self Check

- Birds can fly with the help of their wings. ☐
- Birds have three types of feathers: body, down and flight. ☐
- Birds have different types of beaks according to their feeding habits. ☐
- Birds have different types of claws for digging, running, feeding and other activities. ☐

- Many birds migrate to protect themselves from extremely cold weather. ☐

____

____

Practice

1. What kinds of beaks do the following birds have? What are they used for?

hummingbird ____________________

duck ____________________

sparrow ____________________

robin ____________________

spoonbill ____________________

2. Write T for true and F for false. Correct the false statements.

a. Pigeons have hooked beaks. ☐

b. A woodpecker has a chisel-shaped beak. ☐

c. Eagles have talons. ☐

d. Crows have webbed feet. ☐

3. Answer the following questions.

a. Differentiate between flight feathers and down feathers.

b. What type of feet do ducks and geese have? How are they useful?

c. What are talons?

d. Which one of the following birds does not live in water?

(i) Koel (ii) Duck

(iii) Pelican (d) Swan

e. All of the following are parts of a bird, except

(i) beak (ii) feathers

(iii) wings (iv) gill

f. Can you fly? How do birds fly?

4. Critical Thinking

a. Why do birds have different types of beaks?

b. Birds make nests. Why?

5. Social Emotional Skills

How is the female cuckoo bird different from other female birds? Is it right to do what it does?

6. Creativity

Make a bird feeder with the help of a used plastic bottle.

14 The Human Body

Explore

Which part of your body do you use when you do the following actions:
walk, jump, blink, wink, breathe, smell, chew.

The human body is like a machine or a computer with several different parts. It comprises of a head, neck, torso, two arms and two legs. Each part has a specific function to perform. All the parts of the body must function properly for us to be fit and healthy.

The human body is unique as we can stand erect, walk on two feet, use arms to carry and lift objects, and use our opposing thumbs. The average height of an adult male is about five feet seven inches to five feet eleven inches; while an average adult female is between five feet two inches to five feet seven inches.

An adult human body has 22 internal organs, 600 muscles, approximately 206 bones and about a 100 trillion cells.

All living things are made up of cells. A cell is the basic unit of life. It is the smallest part of our body. Similar cells together form a tissue. Similar tissues join to form an organ. Many organs performing the same function together form an organ system. There are many organ systems in our body to perform different functions.

Cells → Tissues → Organs → Organ systems → Human body

Skeletal System

Circle Time

Have you or any of your family members had a broken bone? Discuss.

If humans did not have bones, we would be floppy like a puppet, unable to walk or even stand up on our own.

The framework of different types of bones is called a skeleton and forms our skeletal system.

The skeleton

- forms a framework that supports the body.
- provides protection, reducing risk of injury to the internal organs.

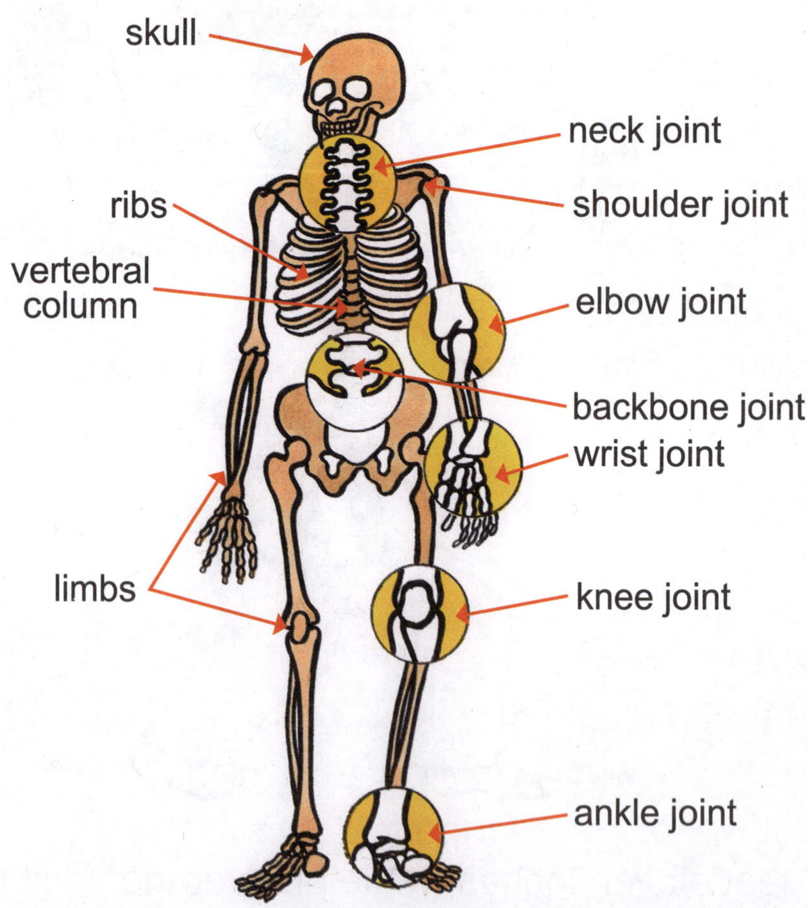

skeletal system

For example, the skull protects the delicate brain inside it.

The body parts that bend are known as **joints**. The joint is the place where two bones meet. We use different joints to move different body parts.

Which joints do you think are used when you do these actions? There may be more than one joint involved in some of these actions.

looking sideways	________	waving goodbye	________
kicking a ball	________	drawing a sketch	________
touching your toes	________	skipping	________

Muscular System

All the muscles together form the muscular system. Muscles are attached to the bones in the body. They allow us to move the different parts of our body. All muscles are made up of elastic tissue (just like the material in a rubber band). Thousands of small tissue fibres make up each muscle.

Muscles in the body are of different kinds.

Digestive System

We eat food such as bread, meat and vegetables to stay alive and be active. However, our body cannot absorb the food in the form that it is consumed. Food and drink need to be broken down into smaller parts so that they can be absorbed into the blood and carried to cells throughout the body. This process of breaking down food into smaller parts is called digestion.

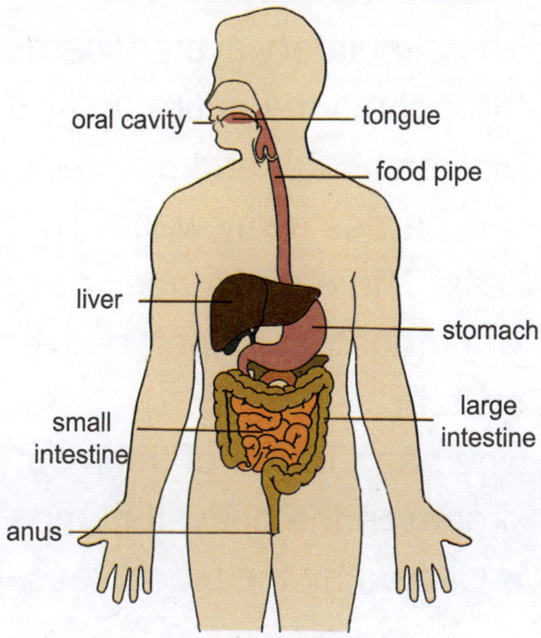

digestive system

The organs that helps us to do this form the digestive system. The teeth, tongue, food pipe, stomach, small intestine and large intestine form the digestive system.

Respiratory System

The parts of our body that help us breathe make up the respiratory system. All cells in the body require oxygen. We breathe in air, which contains oxygen, through the nose. This oxygen is taken to all parts of the body by the blood.

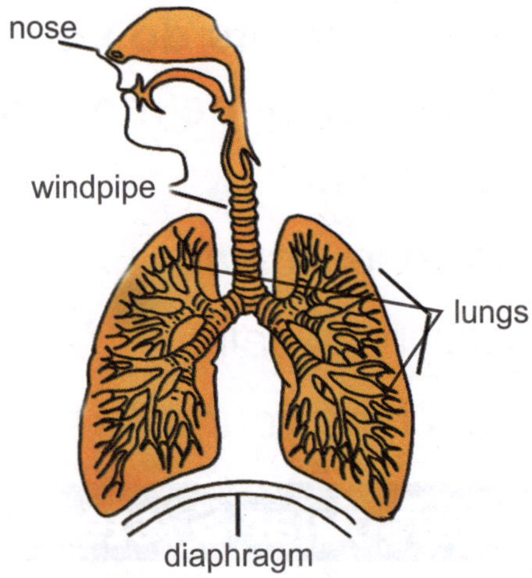

respiratory system

The vital parts of the respiratory system are nose, wind pipe, lungs and diaphragm. The diaphragm is a layer of muscles bellow the lungs. Lungs help us to breathe in oxygen and breathe out carbon dioxide.

Find out how creatures such as whales, that have lungs, can stay underwater for long periods of time.

Circulatory System

The circulatory system carries materials throughout the entire body. It transports oxygen, water and nutrients to the cells and carries away waste produced by the cells. The heart, blood vessels and blood work together as part of the circulatory system.

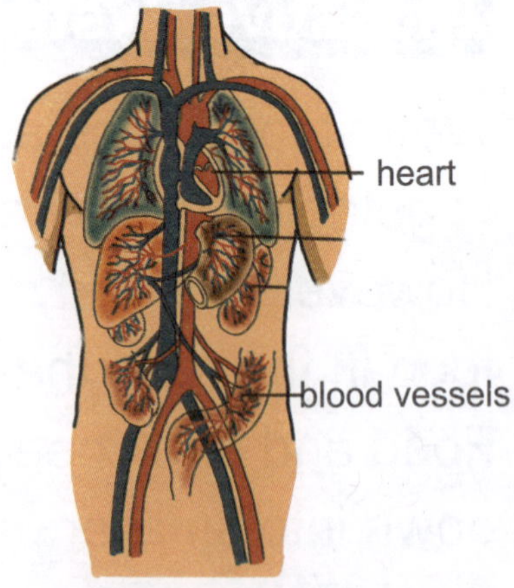

circulatory system

The heart is one of the most important organs in the body. It pumps blood throughout our body. The blood is carried by the blood vessels.

Excretory System

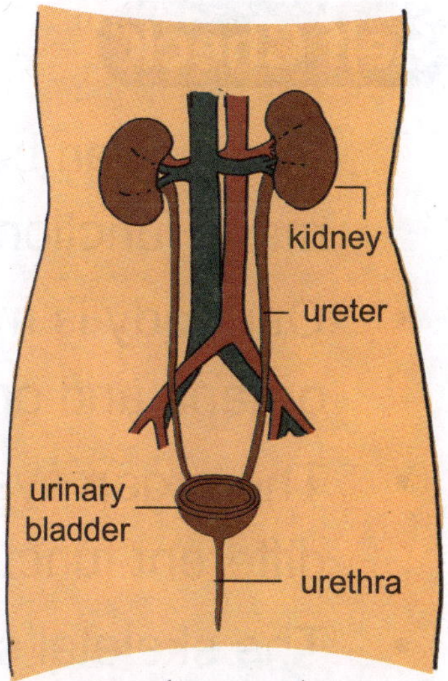

excretory system

The excretory system cleans the body. It helps in removing unwanted things, such as solid waste and liquid waste, in the form of urine and sweat, from the body. The organs included in the excretory system are kidneys, urinary bladder, urethra, skin and parts of the digestive and respiratory systems.

Nervous System

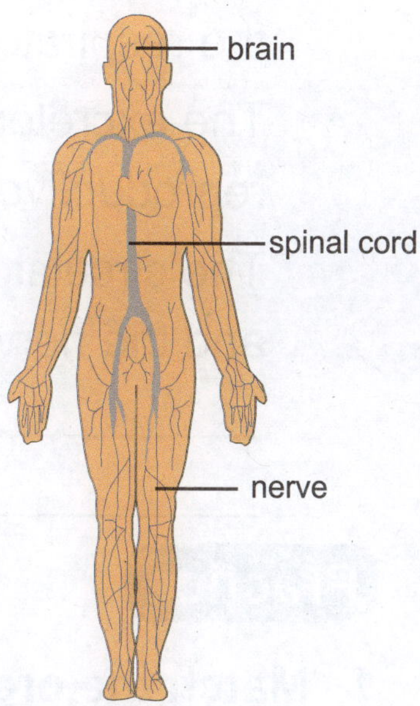

nervous system

The nervous system is the control centre of the body. It controls all actions and reactions of our body. The brain has messengers known as **nerves**. They send instructions to the muscles, bones and so on, telling them what to do. Nerves also carry messages from the body to the brain. The brain, spinal cord and nerves make up our nervous system.

Reproductive System

The reproductive system is made up of organs that produce young ones.

Learn More

Find out what is meant by indigestion.

nerves: bundles of fibres that help to convey information between the brain and other parts of the body

Self Check

- The human body is like a machine which performs many functions. ☐
- Our body is made up of cells which form tissues, organs and organ systems. ☐
- The organ systems help us to perform different functions. ☐
- The skeletal system consists of bones, while the muscular system comprises of muscles. Both these systems help in movement. ☐
- Our digestive system helps in digestion, and the respiratory system helps in breathing. ☐
- The excretory system cleans the body, and the reproductive system helps in producing young ones. ☐
- The circulatory system helps in blood circulation, and the nervous system controls all the actions. ☐

____

____

Practice

1. Match the organ to its system.

heart •	• respiratory system
lungs •	• circulatory system
skull •	• nervous system
kidneys •	• digestive system
muscles •	• skeletal system
intestines •	• muscular system
brain •	• excretory system

2. **Find these body parts in the grid. You need to look across, down and diagonally.**

heart	neck	blood	nose	lungs	bones
brain	muscles	mouth	stomach	bladder	

b	r	a	i	n	c	b	o	n	e	s
x	h	z	x	y	d	l	z	o	a	q
y	n	e	c	k	e	o	z	s	b	y
z	f	g	a	q	z	o	q	e	c	m
h	i	j	k	r	u	d	x	h	b	o
l	m	n	o	p	t	v	c	q	l	u
l	u	n	g	s	w	a	q	z	a	t
q	r	s	q	y	m	x	z	p	d	h
t	v	y	z	o	q	d	u	u	d	z
u	x	z	t	b	c	e	x	v	e	x
m	u	s	c	l	e	s	z	w	r	y

3. **Answer the following questions.**

a. What is an organ system? List the various organ systems.

b. What are nerves?

c. Write the functions of the following organ systems:

(i) skeletal system

(ii) digestive system

(iii) circulatory system

(iv) respiratory system

d. The organs which are like the electric wiring in our body are__________ .

(i) nerves (ii) intestines

(iii) tongue (iv) fingers

e. Kailash plays cricket. Which body systems help him to run, jump and hit the ball?

(i) skeletal (ii) muscular

(iii) excretory (iv) both (i) and (ii)

f. How do broken bones get healed?

4. Critical Thinking

a. Why is the heart one of the most important organs in our body?

b. Why should we chew our food properly?

5. Social Emotional Skills

How does an organ system work? Have you ever worked in a team? What are the benefits of working in a team?

6. Creativity

On a chart paper, list the parts of your body used while doing the following activities:

Activities	Parts of body		
	Internal organs	External organs	Organ system
Breathing			
Eating			
Running			
Reading			

15 Food

Explore

Classify the food items below as healthy or junk food.
Write H for healthy and J for junk in the boxes.

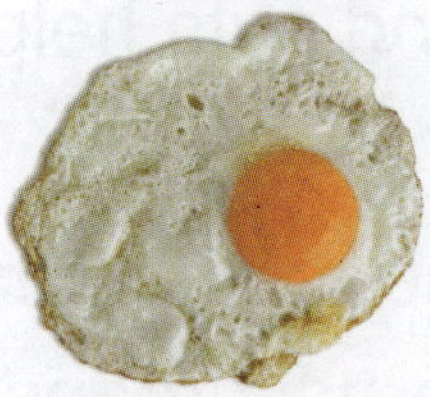

The food that we eat provides us with the energy to study, work, play and remain active. We also need food to grow and to remain healthy.

The food substances which are required by our body are called **nutrients**. All healthy food items have various **nutrients**. A healthy food item might be rich in one or more nutrients.

The following are the important nutrients and food components required by our body:

1. **Carbohydrates** are broken down by our bodies to release energy for work and play. Wheat, rice, potatoes and bread are examples of food rich in carbohydrates.
2. **Vitamins** and **minerals** are found in fruits, vegetables and nuts. These protect us from diseases and give our body the ability to fight against germs and to work efficiently.
3. **Proteins** are body builders and repairers and are particularly important for growth. Fish, milk, eggs, meats and nuts help build muscle strength and are rich sources of proteins.
4. **Fats** keep us warm and give us energy. Cheese, butter, ghee and oil are rich in fats. Fats also protect our internal organs. However, eating extra fat is not good for health.

Roughage and water: Salads, raw vegetables and fruits have lots of fibres. This fibrous substance is called roughage. We need roughage as it helps to remove solid waste from our body.

Water is another vital substance for our body. Three-fourth of our body is made up of water. Water helps in blood circulation, digestion and maintaining body temperature. Water also helps to flush out waste products and **toxins** from our body. Therefore, we should drink plenty of water every day.

toxins: poisonous substances

Balanced Diet

Diet which has all the nutrients in the proper amounts is called balanced diet. Eating a balanced diet means having food from all the food groups in proper proportions in our meals. A balanced diet helps us to grow properly and keeps us healthy, strong and active.

Factastic!

Milk is white because it contains a white protein known as casein. Milk also contains fat, which is also white.

Circle Time

Discuss your favourite food items. Which nutrients do they contain?

Staying Healthy

We need to look after our body to keep it working properly. Remember the following points to stay healthy:

Yoga and other forms of exercise help us stay healthy.

- Eat a balanced diet.
- Exercise daily. Exercise is good for the heart and muscles, and it also keeps the joints flexible.
- Sleep at least eight hours in a day. Sound sleep of eight hours gives the body a chance to rest and repair itself.
- Drink 8 to 10 glasses of water through the day.
- Keep germs away. Germs can make you ill.
- Wash your hands before eating and after going to the toilet.

Foodborne Illnesses

Sometimes the food we eat makes us ill. This condition is known as food poisoning. Food poisoning occurs when we eat food containing germs. Spoilt or raw meat, and raw and unwashed fruits and vegetables may contain **germs**. To avoid food poisoning, we need to wash, cook and store food properly. Certain food items, like cereals, pulses and some vegetables, cannot be eaten raw, and need to be cooked first. Cooking:

– makes the food tasty.

– makes food easy to chew and digest.

– kills the germs present in raw food.

Name a few methods of cooking food.

________________ ________________

________________ ________________

Learn More

Eating from only one food group or eating too much junk food may make you unwell and unhealthy. Find out the other problems one may face by making unhealthy food choices.

Self Check

- Food gives us energy and keeps us healthy and strong. ☐
- Nutrients are useful substances present in food. ☐
- We need proteins for the growth and repair of our body. ☐
- Vitamins and minerals protect us from diseases. ☐
- Carbohydrates and fats give us energy to work and play. ☐
- We should eat enough roughage and drink plenty of water to remain healthy. ☐

germs: harmful microorganisms that cause illness

- A balanced diet has all the nutrients in the correct proportions. ☐
- To stay healthy, we need to eat a balanced diet, take proper rest and exercise. ☐

____

____

Practice

1. Give two examples of each.

a. protein rich foods ______________ ______________

b. foods that provide energy __________ __________

c. foods that contain minerals and vitamins _______ _______

2. Fill in the blanks to complete the following statements.

a. We must eat from all the ____________.

b. We get most of our food from ____________ and animals.

c. We must ____________ our hands before we eat.

d. We should ____________ for eight hours in a day.

e. We must ____________ our food properly.

3. Answer the following questions.

a. What are nutrients? Give examples.

b. Drinking plenty of water helps us. How?

c. What is a balanced diet?

d. All the food items listed below are rich in proteins, except_____ .

(i) eggs (ii) milk

(iii) meat (iv) cucumber

e. Cereals are an important source of____________ .

(i) proteins (ii) fats

(iii) carbohydrates (iv) vitamins

f. What would happen if you stopped eating green vegetables?

4. **Critical Thinking**

   a. Cereals and pulses should be cooked before eating. Why?

   b. Why should we have a balanced diet?

5. **Social Emotional Skills**

   Why should we eat breakfast? Do you eat breakfast before going to school?

6. **Creativity**

   Track your diet for one day.

   Observe and list all the things you eat. Place them in the correct rows. Are you eating a balanced diet?

	Breakfast	Lunch	Dinner
Carbohydrates			
Fats			
Proteins			
Vitamins and minerals			
Roughage and water			

16 The Universe and the Solar System

Explore

Observe the sky on a clear night and list all that you can see.

The Earth is surrounded by a layer of air. Beyond this is empty space where we see the Sun, the Moon and the stars.
When we look through a telescope, we can see much more of the vast space that is the universe. The word 'universe' means whole or complete, which includes all living as well as non-living things.

The universe contains millions of stars. A big group or a cluster of stars is known as a **galaxy**. There are thousands of galaxies in the universe.

It is believed that 12 or 14 billion years ago, the entire universe was created in a sudden massive explosion called the Big Bang. Use an encyclopedia to find out more about the Big Bang.

Factastic!

In ancient times, it was believed that the objects visible in the sky were part of the heavens. Hence, all the objects in the universe were known as 'heavenly bodies'. This term is used even today when we talk about the Sun, Moon and stars.

When seen from the Earth, groups of stars seem to form patterns. These groups of stars are called constellations. Try to observe such patterns in the sky at night.

Orion constellation

The Solar System

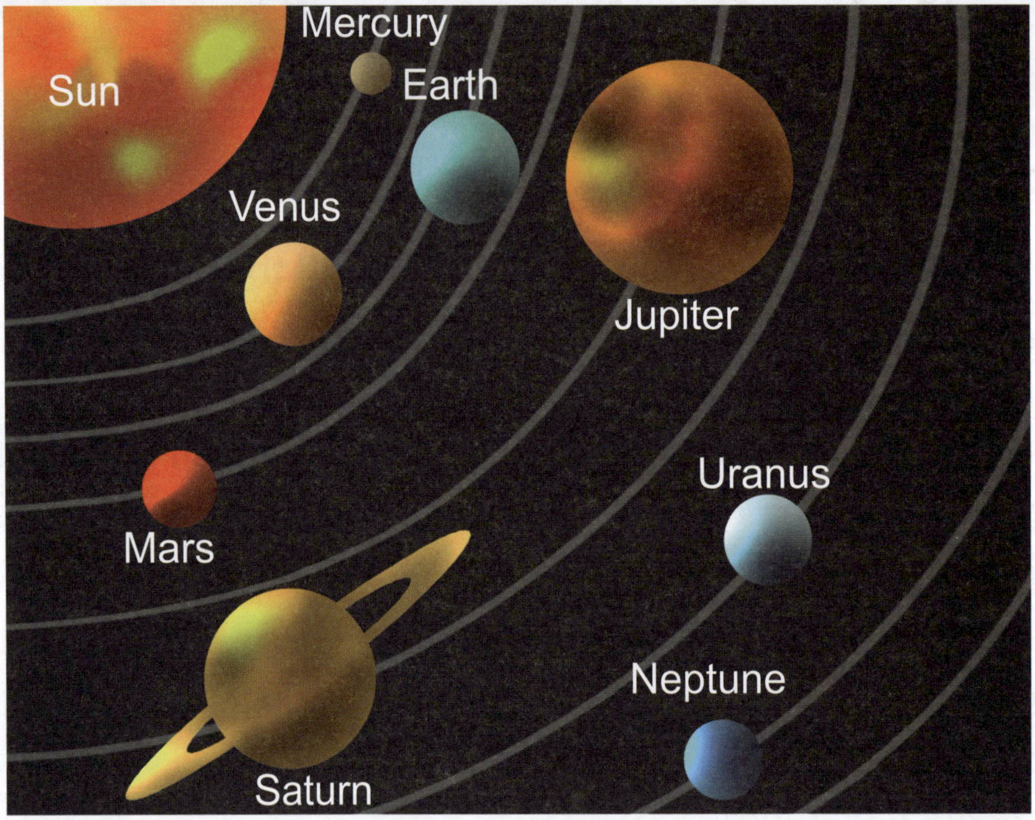

The Solar System is made up of the Sun, which is the central star; the planets that circle it: Mercury, Venus, Earth, Mars, Jupiter, Saturn, Uranus and Neptune; their moons or satellites; as well as dust and pieces of rock. The planets move around the Sun in fixed elliptical paths called orbits. Pluto, earlier considered the ninth planet, is now classified as a dwarf planet. The Solar System is in the Milky Way galaxy.

Satellites

Satellites are objects that move around a planet. These satellites vary in size, shape and number. The Earth has one natural satellite, the Moon.

elliptical path: oval-shaped path

Moon

The Moon is our closest neighbour in the sky. Just as the Earth moves around the Sun, the Moon moves around the Earth. It takes twenty-seven days to complete its orbit around the Earth. This is known as the **lunar cycle**. The Moon also moves around the Sun with the Earth.

The surface of the Moon shows mountains and large bowl-shaped depressions, known as craters. There is no life on the Moon, as it does not have any air or water.

surface of the Moon

The Moon is not a star and does not have any light of its own. The moonlight that we see at night is actually the Sun's light being reflected by the Moon. The Moon is much smaller than the Sun, but it appears to be the same size as it is much close to us.

> **Factastic!**
>
> The Moon rotates once every 27 days, 7 hours and 43.7 minutes and also orbits the Earth once in about 27 days, 7 hours and 43.7 minutes. This is why we always see the same face of the Moon.

The Moon seems to change its shape every night. However, the Moon does not actually change its shape. The visible shape differs because only a part of the moon is illuminated by the Sun.

These different shapes are called the phases of the Moon.

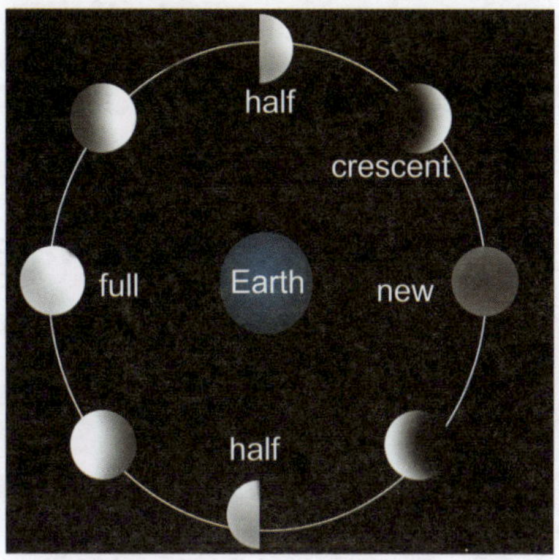

Look at the picture of the globe and colour the surface of the Earth with appropriate colours for land and water.

The Earth

The Earth is the third planet from the Sun. It was formed many, many years ago. The Earth is not a perfect round shape. It is shaped like an orange—a slightly flattened top and bottom and a bulging middle.

The flat end at the top is known as the **North Pole** and the one at the bottom is known as the **South Pole**.

When the Earth was formed, it was a very hot spherical structure and there was no life on it. Rains and thunderstorms cooled down the Earth from outside. Slowly, living forms started to appear on it.

Earth is the only planet where there is life because it is surrounded by a layer of air known as the **atmosphere.** The air that we breathe is a part of the atmosphere. The atmosphere has the correct temperature for living beings to survive; it is neither too hot nor too cold.

The surface of the Earth is made up of land and water. People, plants and animals live on land. Some plants and animals also live under water. Water is very important for the survival of all living beings.

The presence of air, water and the correct temperature makes it possible for life to exist on the Earth.

Rotation and Revolution

All planets and natural satellites have two kinds of movements—rotation and revolution.

axis of rotation

Rotation

Rotation is when a planet or its moon turns all the way around on its **axis.** The Earth also rotates around an axis, known as its rotational axis.

The Earth rotates from the West to the East. It takes twenty-four hours to rotate once. The time it takes for the Earth to complete one rotation is known as one day. As the Earth rotates on its axis, part of the Earth faces the Sun and the other half is away from the Sun. The part facing the Sun has day at that time and the other half, which is away from the Sun, has night. As the Earth spins, we move through the light into the darkness and back again. This results in day and night.

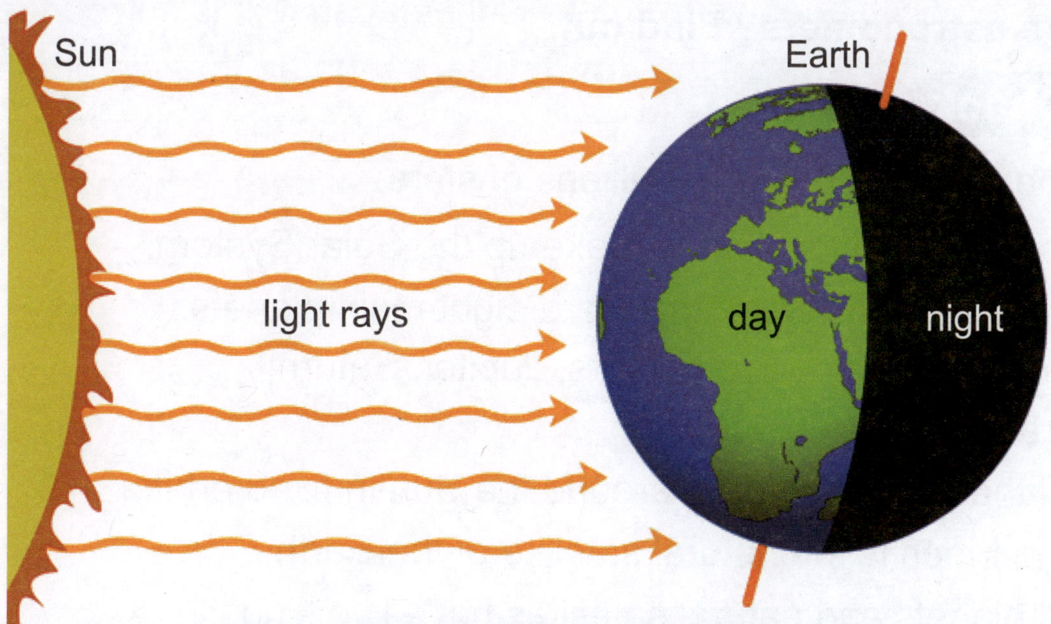

day and night on the Earth

axis: an imaginary line passing through the centre, around which a planet rotates

Revolution

While the Earth spins or rotates on its axis, it also simultaneously moves around the Sun on a fixed path known as its orbit. This movement of a planet around any other object is known as revolution.

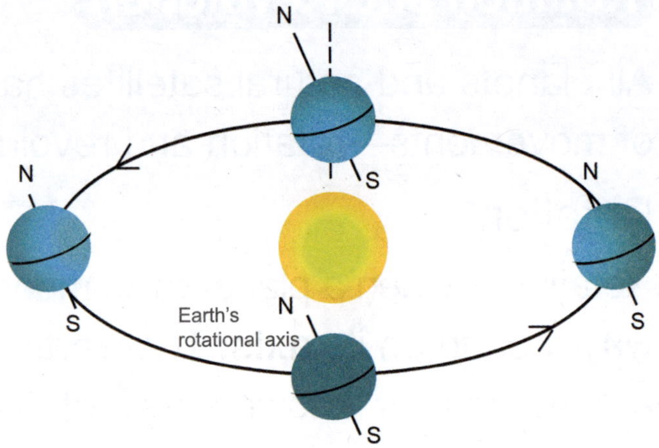

revolution of the Earth

The Earth's orbit is oval or elliptical in shape. The Earth takes $365\frac{1}{4}$ days to complete one revolution around the Sun. The time taken to complete one revolution around the Sun is called a year. So, a year has $365\frac{1}{4}$ days. The revolution of the Earth around the Sun is responsible for the different seasons.

Learn More

Who are astronomers? Find out.

Self Check

- The universe contains millions of stars. ☐
- The Sun and its planets make up the Solar System. ☐
- In the Solar System, there are eight main planets: Mercury, Venus, Earth, Mars, Jupiter, Saturn, Uranus and Neptune ☐
- All the planets revolve around the Sun in fixed orbits. ☐
- The Moon is the natural satellite of the Earth. ☐
- All planets and natural satellites have two kinds of movements: rotation and revolution. ☐
- The rotation of the Earth causes day and night. ☐

Practice

1. Write T for true and F for false. Correct the false statements.

a. An orbit is the path that the Sun moves on.

b. The lunar cycle is of 40 days.

c. A natural satellite is a celestial body that orbits a planet.

d. There is an imaginary line going down from the North Pole to the South Pole.

e. Planets have their own light.

2. Find and colour these words in the grid.

Earth	axis	revolution	Sun	North Pole	planet

r	e	v	o	l	u	t	i	o	n
x	o	y	z	o	z	x	c	f	o
y	z	t	m	e	z	b	d	g	r
z	p	l	a	n	e	t	k	l	t
h	z	x	b	t	t	j	m	n	h
e	a	r	t	h	i	i	v	u	p
y	x	z	e	g	o	o	p	w	o
b	i	d	f	h	p	t	n	x	l
c	s	u	n	q	r	s	y	z	e

3. Answer the following questions.

a. What is the Solar System? Name all the planets of our Solar System.

b. What causes day and night? Explain with the help of a diagram.

c. Differentiate between rotation and revolution of the Earth.

d. The Solar System is part of the __________ .

(i) Light Way (ii) Milky Way

(iii) Andromeda (iv) Big bear

e. Most planets move along me as they revolve around the Sun. I am fixed and normally elliptical. Who am I?

(i) axis (ii) orbit (iii) equator (iv) latitude

f. What would happen if the Earth stops rotating on its axis?

4. Critical Thinking

a. Why do you think the Moon shines at night?

b. Life exists only on Earth. Why?

5. Social Emotional Skills

Can we see a clear sky in big cities these days?

Why is it so? Discuss.

6. Creativity & Information literacy

Identify the people in the following pictures. Collect information about their achievements and display.

__________ __________ __________

__________ __________ __________

__________ __________ __________

17 Natural Resources

Explore

Make a list of things we use every day that are not made by humans.

Natural resources are substances which are not man-made. These are found in or on the Earth's crust and in oceans, forests and mountains. Oil, coal, natural gas, metals and minerals are all examples of natural resources. Other examples are air, water, sunlight, soil, plants, animals, birds and aquatic life. They are either living or support life and meet our needs.

Fuels, such as coal and petroleum, are also natural resources.

Rock and Soil

Visit a garden and collect some soil. What do you see in it?

Soil is the topmost layer of the Earth's crust. Soil is formed by the breaking of rocks into small pieces over a long period of time. Plants obtain minerals from the soil. Soil is made up of mineral particles, water, air and living organisms, as well as non-living material. Soil contains gravel, sand, clay and humus. The topmost layer has dead leaves, twigs and decomposed parts of dead animals, which make it very fertile and good for growing plants. This is called humus.

On the basis of the size of the soil particles, there are three types of soils–sandy, clayey and loamy.

Clayey soil is made up of fine and smooth soil particles which make it sticky. It holds a lot of water and little air.

Sandy soil is made up of bigger soil particles. This type of soil can not hold much water.

Loamy soil is a mixture of sandy and clayey soil. It can hold both water and air, therefore it is a good soil for growing plants.

Collect some soil in a jar. Add water, close the jar and shake it well. Leave it for an hour and record your observation.
What is soil profile? Find out.

Rocks are found everywhere on the Earth's surface and under the ground. There are different kinds of rocks. Rocks such as marble, granite and sandstone are used to make buildings, while diamonds, rubies and emeralds are used in jewellery.

Rocks break up into very small pieces to form soil particles. Different kinds of rocks make up different kinds of soil.

Most rocks contain minerals. Metals are extracted from these minerals. Iron, copper, gold and silver are a few examples of metals.

precious stones

- Metals are usually shiny solids.
- Metals allow heat and electricity to pass through them.
- Metals can be formed into sheets and wires.

Fuels such as coal and petroleum are also natural resources. Crude oil is found under the ground and under the seabed. It is refined to make petrol, kerosene, plastic and so on.

Make a list of metals used at your home. Which is the most expensive metal? Why is it so expensive? Find out.

Water

We can survive without food for upto two to three weeks, but we cannot survive without water for more than three days.

We use water every day for various activities at home. More than three-fourths of the Earth's surface is covered by water. Water is present in the oceans, seas, rivers, lakes and ponds and also under ground. It is also present as ice in glaciers and as water vapour in the air. All life on the Earth depends on water for survival.

glacier

Plants

Plants produce oxygen as a by-product of the process of photosynthesis. We depend on plants for oxygen and for food. We eat different parts of plants, such as fruits, flowers, stems, leaves and roots. Wood from trees is used to make wooden furniture, cupboards and wooden flooring in our homes. We also obtain oils, rubber and medicines from plants.

glacier: a slow-moving mass of ice formed by the accumulation and compression of snow over several years

Air

Air is all around us. However, we cannot see it. We can only feel air. Air is made up of different gases, mainly nitrogen, oxygen and carbon dioxide, along with water vapour.

Oxygen in the air is necessary for respiration and combustion, while carbon dioxide is used by green plants to prepare food.

Can you find out other uses of air?

Learn More

Some natural resources are depleting fast. Find out some ways to save them.

Self Check

- The resources we obtain from nature are called natural resources; for example air, water, coal, plants and soil. ☐
- The topmost layer of the Earth's crust is called soil. ☐
- Soil is made up of rock, gravel, sand, clay and humus. ☐
- Metals are extracted from minerals. ☐
- Air consists of gases, mainly nitrogen, oxygen, carbon dioxide, along with water vapour and dust particles. ☐
- Plants prepare food for us. ☐
- We need oxygen, water and food to survive. ☐
- We need to use our natural resources judiciously. ☐

____

____

respiration: inhalation and exhalation of air; breathing
combustion: the process of burning

Practice

1. Name five things that live in the soil and draw any two.

____

____

____

____

____

2. Fill in the blanks with the correct words from the brackets.

a. ____________ is a natural resource.
(Plastic/Metal/Building)

b. ____________ gas is released during photosynthesis.
(Oxygen/Carbon dioxide/Nitrogen)

c. __________ are used in jewellery.
(Rubies/Soil/Plants)

d. __________ is the topmost layer of the Earth's crust.
(Coal/Soil/Mineral)

e. Different __________ make different soils.
(rocks/gases/plants)

3. Answer the following questions.

a. What are natural resources? Name any four.

b. What is soil? How is it formed?

c. What are the various sources of water?

d. Pick the odd one out.

(i) Silver (ii) Copper

(iii) Gold (iv) Diamond

e. Which of these is not one of the main components of the air all around us?

(i) Oxygen (ii) Nitrogen

(iii) Carbon dioxide (iv) Sulphur dioxide

f. Is soil living or non-living thing?

4. Critical Thinking

a. Humus is important for plant growth. Why?

b. Why do we need air?

5. Social Emotional Skills

Discuss ways to keep the air clean.

6. Creativity

Colour the objects made from metals.

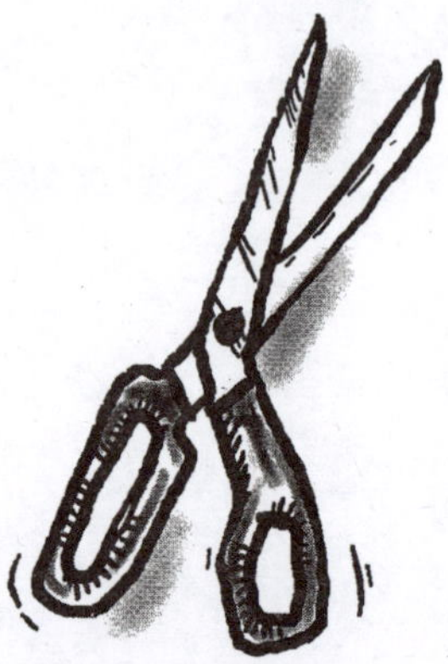

18 Matter and Its Properties

Explore

Spill water in an open area of the classroom and observe what happens. Note that the water goes everywhere and spreads on the floor. Remember to mop up the water later.

What happens when you drop a book on the floor? Does it spread on the floor like the water? Yes ☐ No ☐

All objects have certain properties:

1. **Objects take up space**. All the objects around you in your classroom, such as books, tables, chairs and pencils, take up space. The amount of space occupied by an object is called its volume.
2. **Objects have mass**. Mass is how much there is of a substance. It is related to how much that object weighs.

Anything that occupies space and has mass is called **matter**. Everything around us is made up of matter. Some objects may be heavy, while others may be light. This is because different objects have different mass. Mass tells us how heavy or light an object is.

Matter exists in three different forms: solid, liquid and gas. These three forms are also called **states of matter**.

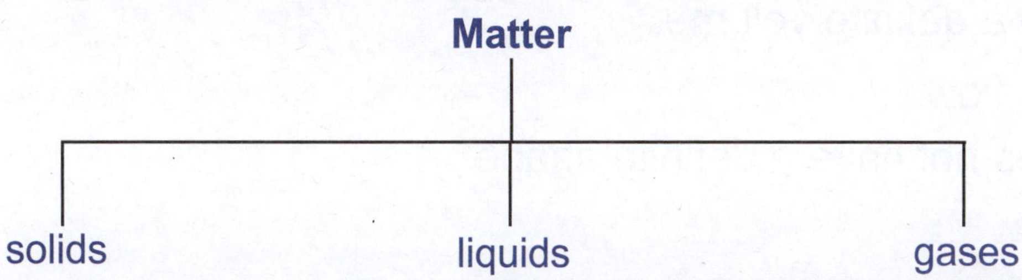

Solid

Matter in its solid state has a fixed shape.

For example, a block of wood has a fixed shape and size. Solids do not change their shape when moved to another container.

A solid has the following properties:

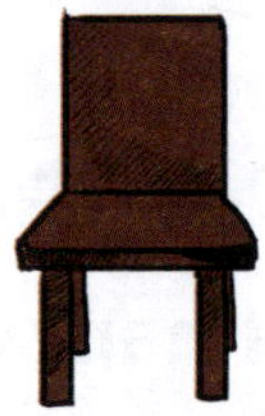

- It has a definite shape.
- It has a definite mass.
- It has a definite volume.

The shape of a solid can be changed only by cutting or burning it.

Liquid

Matter in its liquid state takes the shape of the container in which it is kept. Liquids can flow, can be poured and even spilled.

Water is a liquid. It occupies space and, therefore, has volume. It takes the shape of the container in which it is kept.

A liquid has the following properties:

- It has a definite mass.
- It has a definite volume.
- It can flow.
- It does not have a definite shape.

volume: the amount of space occupied by a substance or object

Gas

Observe what happens when water is boiled and water vapour is formed. Does water vapour have any shape? Yes ☐ No ☐

A gas is a state of matter which has no fixed shape or volume. It occupies the entire space available. A gas has the following properties:

- no definite shape
- no definite volume
- occupies all the space available

Air is a mixture of different gases like nitrogen, oxygen and carbon dioxide. We feel the air all around us, although we cannot see it. Air also contains water vapour—water in its gaseous state.

Change in the States of Matter

Keep some ice cubes outside the refrigerator and observe the changes.

Matter can change from one state to another. These changes can happen on heating or cooling.

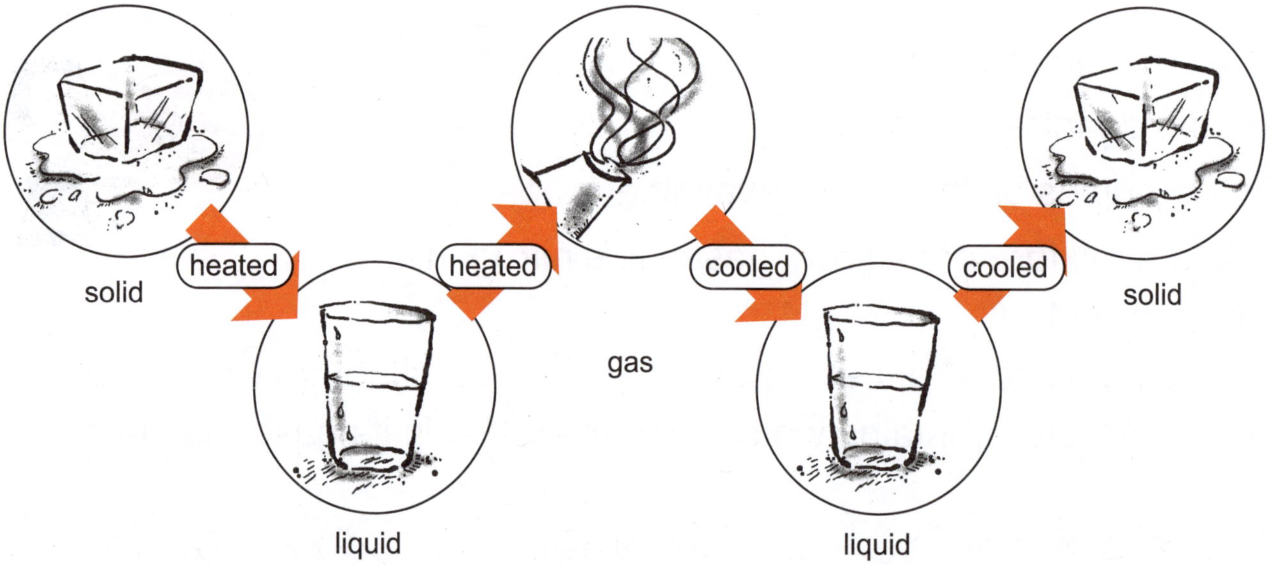

Ice cubes change into water when kept outside the refrigerator due to the warmth in the room.

The process of changing from a solid to a liquid state on heating is called **melting**.

When we heat water, it changes into water vapour. This process of changing from a liquid to a gaseous state on heating is called **evaporation**.

When a gas changes to a liquid state on cooling, the process is called **condensation**.

All these changes are also found in the water cycle.

In the water cycle, ice or snow changes to water on melting and then evaporates to form water vapour due to the heat of the Sun.

Clouds are formed when water vapour condenses on cool dust particles higher up in the atmosphere. Water keeps on changing its state during the entire water cycle.

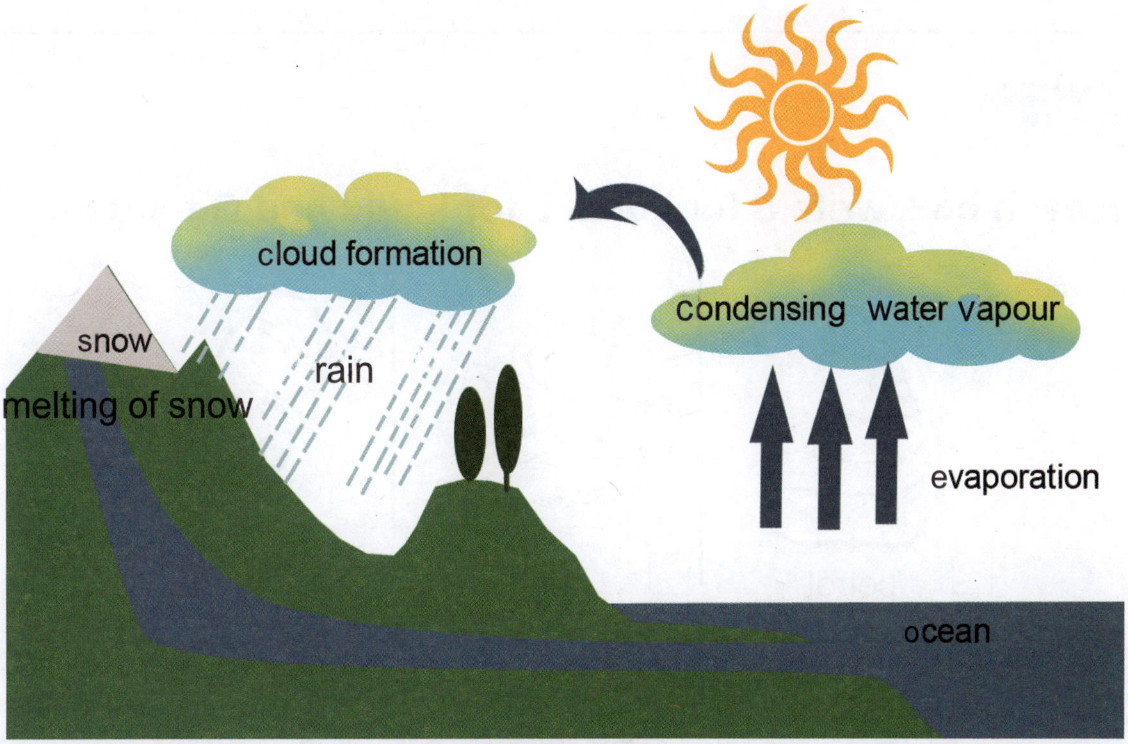

water cycle

Learn More

Imagine you have found some water in your classroom. Find out how this water might be part of the water cycle.

Self Check

- Anything that occupies space and has mass is called matter. ☐
- Everything around us is matter. ☐
- Matter exist in three states—solid, liquid, gas. ☐
- Solids have fixed shape and volume. ☐
- Liquids do not have fixed shape, but have fixed volume. ☐
- Liquids can flow. ☐

- Gases neither have fixed shape nor fixed volume. ☐
- Matter changes its state on heating or cooling. ☐

____

____

Practice

1. In each box, write S for solid, L for liquid and G for gas.

☐ petrol

☐ wind

☐ ice cream

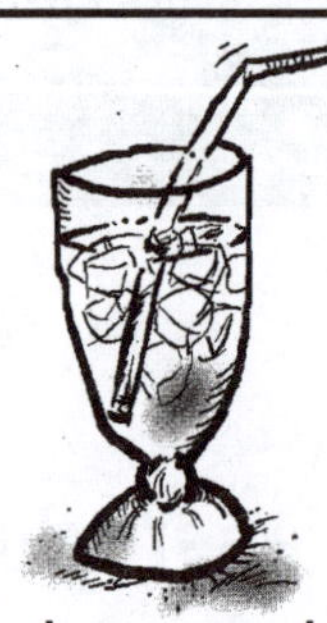

☐ lemonade

☐ flower

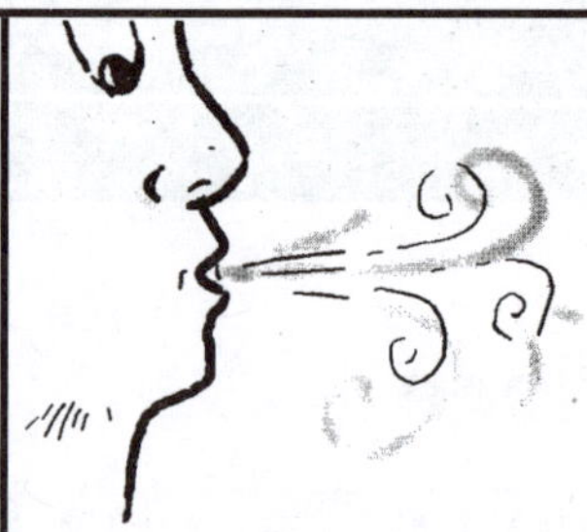

☐ our breath

2. Write T for true and F for false. Correct the false statements.

a. Anything that has mass is matter.

b. Air occupies space.

c. Water has no definite shape, therefore, it is not matter.

d. You cannot change the shape of a solid.

e. Air will expand to fill the space it is kept in.

3. Answer the following questions.

a. What is matter? Name the three states of matter.

b. Write three properties of gases.

c. Name five liquids that are used in our homes. What are they used for?

d. Which of the following is an example of matter?

(i) Mango juice (ii) Bread

(iii) Oxygen (iv) All of these

e. Which of the following will flow?

(i) Plastic (ii) Iron

(iii) Milk (iv) Oxygen

f. What is your physical state? Are you solid, liquid or gas?

4. Critical Thinking

a. A block of wood is solid. Why is it so?

b. When your mother is cooking food in the kitchen, you can smell the food in the other room as well. Why?

5. Social Emotional Skills

List any five liquids which you should not drink.

6. Creativity

Observe the activities done in your kitchen. Make a table and write two examples of the following changes:

Evaporation	Condensation	Melting
1. ______	1. ______	1. ______
2. ______	2. ______	2. ______

19 Energy and Force

Explore

Look at the pictures and tick the appropriate boxes.

pushed ☐

pulled ☐

pushed ☐

pulled ☐

pushed ☐

pulled ☐

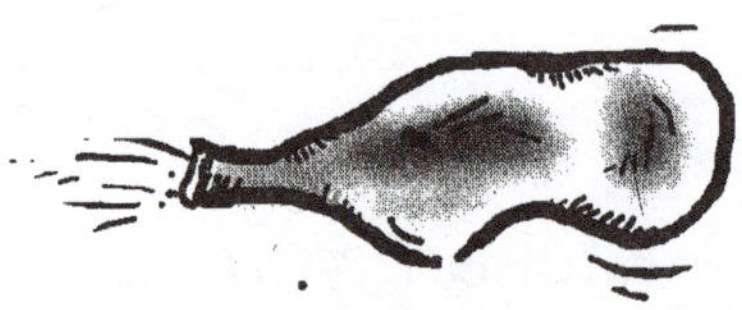

pushed ☐

pulled ☐

pushed ☐

pulled ☐

pushed ☐

pulled ☐

Force

Force means either a push or a pull.

When you play a game of bowling, the ball exerts a **pushing force** against the ten pins, as it strikes them down.

Look at the picture. What is the man doing?

Is he applying a pushing force or a pulling force? ___________________

Although we cannot see force, we can see and feel its effect on things. The balloon in the picture is affected by force as it is moving up.

Force helps us to do many things.

We can push an object.

We can change the shape of objects.

In a game of cricket, as the ball is hit by a bat, it speeds up and changes its direction. Therefore, force can make things speed up and change direction as well.

Force can make things slow down or come to a complete stop.

Force can also make things turn.

Different Types of Forces

There are many different types of forces, such as, force of gravity, friction, muscular force etc.

Air and water also apply force.

- What happens when you jump up?
- What happens to ripe mangoes on trees?
- What happens when you throw a ball up in the air?

Everything that goes up must come down. When you jump up, you come down; fruits ripen and fall to the ground; when you throw a ball up, it eventually comes down. The reason for this is **gravity**. Gravity is a force that the Earth exerts on objects, pulling them downwards, towards the centre of the Earth.

Energy

Can you do work without eating food? For how long can you live without eating food? Discuss.

We all need food to gain energy. Energy is the ability to do work. We will not be able to do work if we do not have energy. There are different forms of energy. Food has chemical energy. Light, sound and heat are other forms of energy.

Light

Can you see objects in a dark room? Shine a torch through a straight pipe. The light will be visible at the other end of the tube. Now, shine the torch through a bent pipe.

Can you see any light shine from the other end of the pipe?

Yes ☐ **No** ☐

Our eyes need light to see objects. Light carries information from the world to our eyes and brains.

The main source of heat and light on the Earth is the Sun.

The flame of a candle, a lamp or a matchstick also gives us light. Such objects which have light of their own are called luminous objects.

Non-luminous objects do not have light of their own.

Examples of **non-luminous** objects are book, glass and table. We cannot see non-luminous objects unless light falls on them. The Moon is also a non-luminous object as it does not have its own light. We see it because it reflects the Sun's light.

Properties of Light

- Light travels in straight lines.
- A shadow is formed when an object blocks the path of light. It is formed on the opposite side of the light source.

Sound

Pluck a string of a guitar. Do you feel the vibrations?

As the string of the guitar vibrates, it creates sound. Sound is a type of energy made by vibrations. When any object vibrates, it causes movement in the air particles. These particles bump into the particles close to them, which makes them vibrate too. This movement, known as sound waves, continues until the particles run out of energy. If your ear is within range of the vibrations, you hear the sound. We can make sounds by clapping our hands, shouting or banging a table.

Factastic!

All musical instruments produce sound because of vibrations. The difference between noise and music is that music is organized into patterns that have pitch and rhythm. Noise has no pattern. It is not organized.

Colour the things whose sounds you like to listen to. Circle those sounds you don't like to hear.

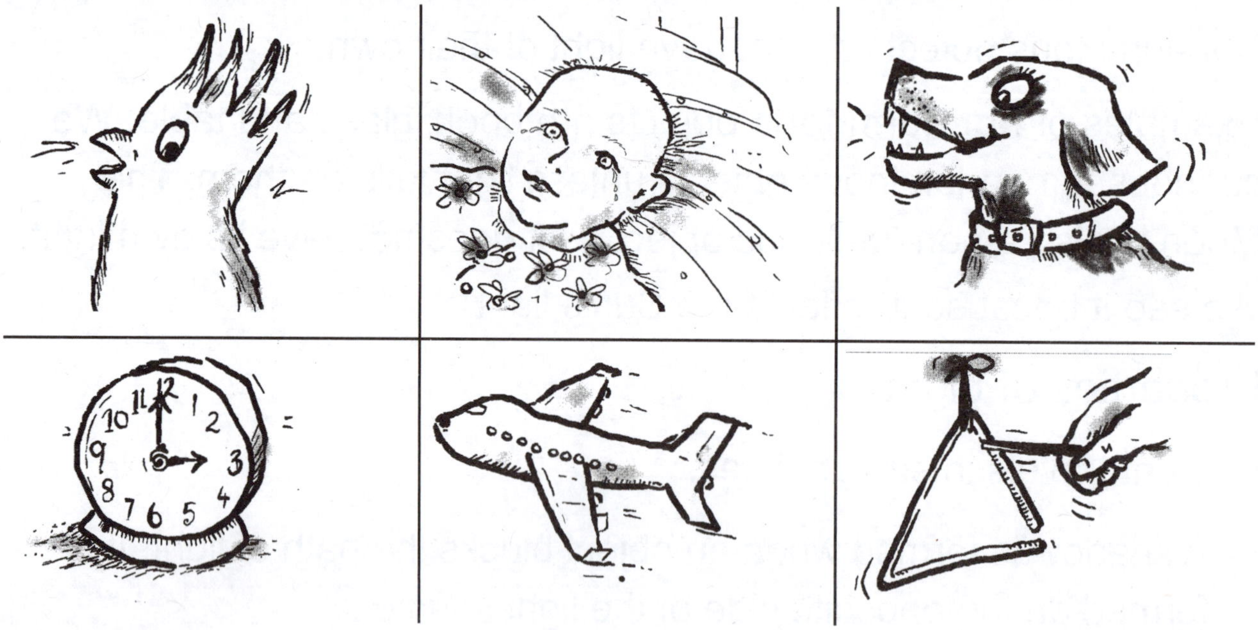

Learn More

Stand in the Sun on a concrete surface once every hour for five hours. Stand at the same spot every time. Ask your friend to trace your shadow with a piece of chalk. Observe the change in the length and position of your shadow as the day progresses.

Self Check

- Force means applying a push or a pull to move or change the shape of any object.
- Force can also make moving objects stop or speed up.
- It can change the direction of movement as well.
- There are different types of force.
- Energy is the ability to do work.
- There are different forms of energy.

Practice

1. Draw an arrow to show the direction in which the baby's cart will move.

1. 

2. 

3. 

4. 

2. Write T for true and F for false. Correct the false statements.

a. Force can make a moving object change its direction.

b. Things at rest will start moving by themselves.

c. Force is a push or a pull.

d. Wind and water both exert force.

e. To generate force, we must have energy.

3. Answer the following questions.

a. What is force? What are its effects?

b. What is energy? Name the different forms of energy.

c. Name four things that make a sound in the classroom, in the school bus, at home and in the playground.

d. Sound is produced by ___________ .

(i) particles (ii) vibrations (iii) force (iv) energy

e. I squeeze, I stretch, I push, I pull,
I make things move; who am I?

(i) Energy (ii) Muscles

(iii) Force (iv) Friction

f. What would happen if you jump in space?

4. Critical Thinking

a. Why is the Moon a non luminous object?

b. Ripe fruits fall down from the tree. Why?

5. Social Emotional Skills

Do you think loud music or loud speakers should be played at night? Discuss.

6. Creativity

Make different shapes with the help of clay. Do you need to apply force? Which effect of force do you observe during this activity?

Cross-curricular Project

Food Around India

1. **In India, people from different states follow different traditions. Traditions are things that we do since many years, on special days.**

   Ask your parents/grandparents about a traditional food item from your state. For example, it could be poha from Madhya Pradesh, momos from Sikkim or chaat from Delhi.

   Write down the ingredients and recipe of this simple dish or drink from your state.

RECIPE

Ingredients: ____________________

Directions: ____________________

2. **Write down the essential nutrient of all the ingredients you have used. This shows you how healthy our recipe is. For example, if you're making poha, rice has carbohydrates.**

Ingredient	Nutrient

What does your dish look like once ready? Draw or paste a picture.

3. **Ask 5 friends what special food their parents or grandparents make during festivals. One is done for you.**

Name	Festival	Name of the dish
1. **Ragini**	**Diwali**	**Kheer and Poori**
2.		
3.		
4.		
5.		
6.		

4. Fill up the health chart for one week. Did you have a healthy week? How can you make it better?

Healthy Routine	Monday	Tuesday	Wednesday	Thursday	Friday	Saturday	Sunday
 What time did you wake up?							
 Did you bathe?							
 What did you eat for breakfast?							
 Did you exercise?							
 How many glasses of water did you drink?							
 What fruits and vegetables did you eat today?							
 What time did you got to bed?							

How to Use an Atlas

A collection of maps compiled into an easy-to-use format is called an atlas. An atlas is a widely used resource in any classroom. Maps help us to identify and locate places around the world, learn more about the settings of stories, understand the historical and newsworthy locations and even do distance calculations. Atlases may be general and cover the entire globe, or they may be specific to geographical locations, topics or time periods. An atlas can have maps detailing the physical and political features, tourist spots, climate, natural resources, the land, sea and air routes.

All maps are reduced to fit the size of the page, according to a scale. The two main types of maps according to scale are:

Large scale maps, which show great details of a small area. For example, the map of a city.

Small scale maps, which provide general information of a large area. For example, the map of a country.

North is depicted at the top of all maps. Most maps have a grid of lines which helps to locate the place. Parallels are lines that represent distances north and south of the Equator. Meridians are lines representing east and west of the Prime Meridian.

An atlas usually has an index at the end of the book. The index is an alphabetical listing of place names and their pronunciations. It gives you longitude and latitude coordinates as well.

Suppose you have to locate INDORE. Look up place name in the index. It may be given as INDORE 13 D4. Go to page 13 and locate INDORE in the grid box D4.

For teachers

A. Display a large map in your classroom. Every morning when students come, write the 'Find Out' or a 'Question of the Day' related to the map.

Questions may include:

How many states border Maharashtra?

Through which states does the Ganga River flow?

In which part of the world is Kenya?

B. Ask the students to create a map of their neighbourhood or colony. Encourage them to use their own keys or symbols. It will be interesting to see what each student chooses as an icon for the legend.

Tips

- Use atlases that are up to date. States and countries sometimes change names and borders. For example, what was once Czechoslovakia (one country) is now Czech Republic and Slovakia (two countries). Similarly, if you are using a road atlas for directions, make sure it is a recent one.
- Study the key or symbol guide to the maps. Each atlas uses different symbols. Symbols are important to know what you are looking for on the maps.
- Use the table of contents to find maps for your research.

How to Use an Encyclopedia

An encyclopedia is a useful resource found in all libraries. An encyclopedia may be a single volume, subject specific, or multi-volume covering a wide range of topics. Because encyclopedias are so easy to use and so accessible, many people use encyclopedias as their first option for a reference tool.

Most general encyclopedias are multivolume sets and are set up in alphabetical format. Some encyclopedias may need you to know the key word or subject heading in order to find specific information covered over a variety of volumes. Some encyclopedias devote separate volumes to different subjects.

Locate the index. The index is usually in the last series of volumes and is in alphabetical order. It gives you page numbers and volume numbers to locate the article you are researching.

Read the article and pick out relevant information for your project.

For teachers

A. Pass a volume of an encyclopedia to a group of students. Ask them to go through the layout, the way the information is organized and the quickest way to locate an entry. Challenge each group to compile an encyclopedia on any topic. Topics could be children's authors, unique inventions, historical sites in Asia, etc.

B. Ask the students to read an entry on any animal of their choice. Encourage the students to write a newspaper article or a poem using all the details and facts from the entry.

Pink is my nose

I thrive on garbage

Go away, my friend

Tips

- Look out for other cross-references that can broaden your topic and provide new insight into your research.
- Pay attention to the maps, graphs and pictures in the article.
- The outline, provided for long articles, is a helpful reference tool when organizing your writing.
- Refer to authors correctly. The information on authors is either in the introductory material or in the index.

How to Use the Internet

One of the most recent and popular resources for research is the Internet. The Internet is a repository of information collected from various sources. Navigating through sites and links can give you updated information. Though the Internet has a wealth of information, before proceeding on any topic, take an adult's help to determine which sites might be reliable and which might not.

Tips

- It is a good idea to sit with an adult and bookmark the sites that you will need for research. This way you can directly go to the pages you want to view.
- Before beginning the topic, write down some keywords on which you will base your research.
- Use quality, child-friendly search engines, such as www.ajkids.com (Ask Jeeves Kids) and www.yahooligans.com (Yahooligans!). You can keep a list of helpful sites near the computer for easy access.
- Quotation marks are important while conducting a topic search. If you enter your topic or key words without quotation marks around it, the search will give information about anything linked to the words. If you put the search topic in quotation marks, you will get information related to the exact words placed within quotation marks.
- If you can't read through the entire article, you can use the FIND option to locate a particular word in the article.

For teachers

A. Divide the class into four groups. Give three groups a topic to research. Each of these groups will have to research from different sources. The fourth group will then review the depth and breadth of the information collected by each, and survey and compare all the sources. It can base its report on:

Which source gave the maximum amount of more information?

Which source gave the better information?

Maps for Practice

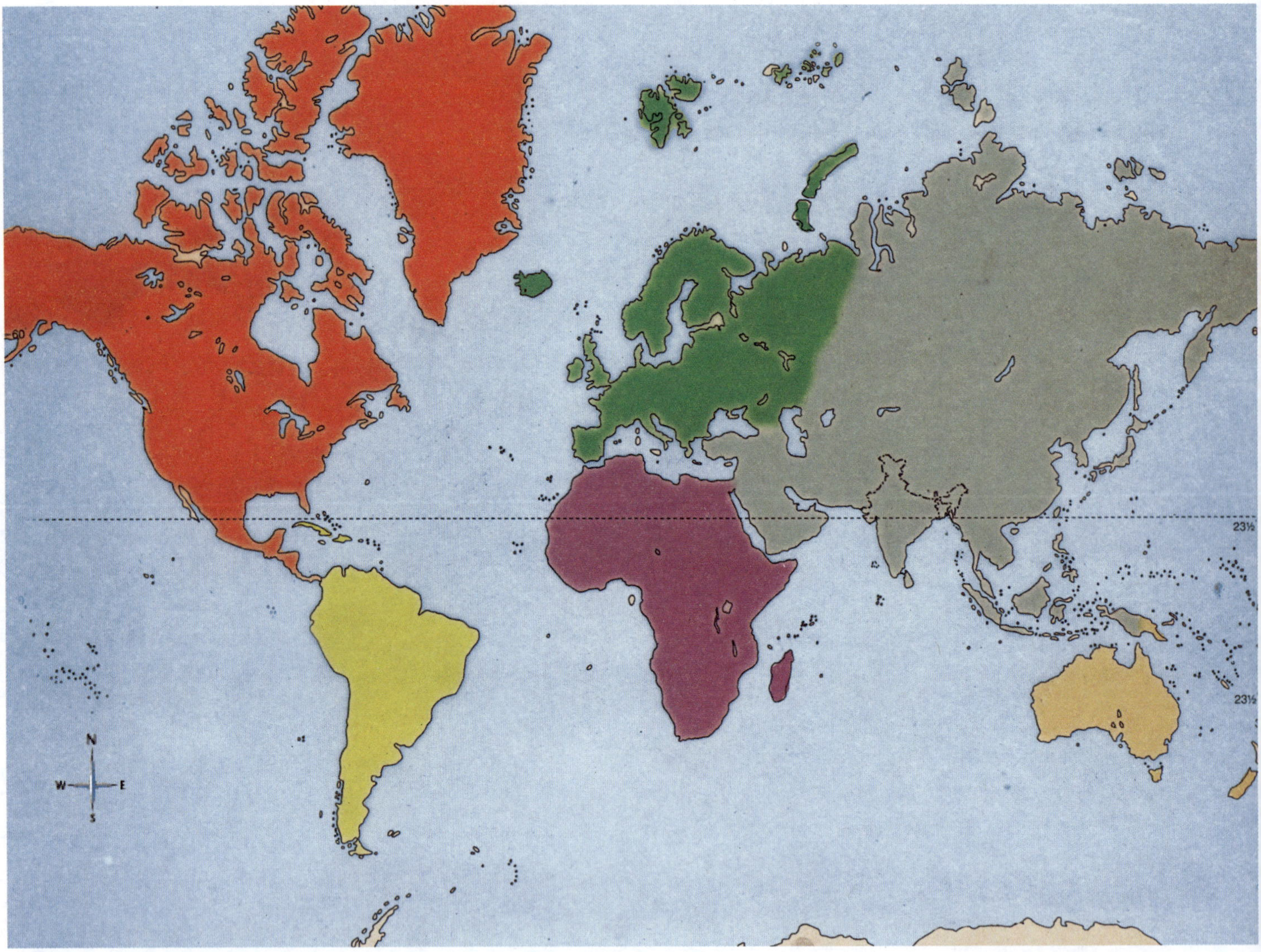
60
23½
23½
N
W
E
S

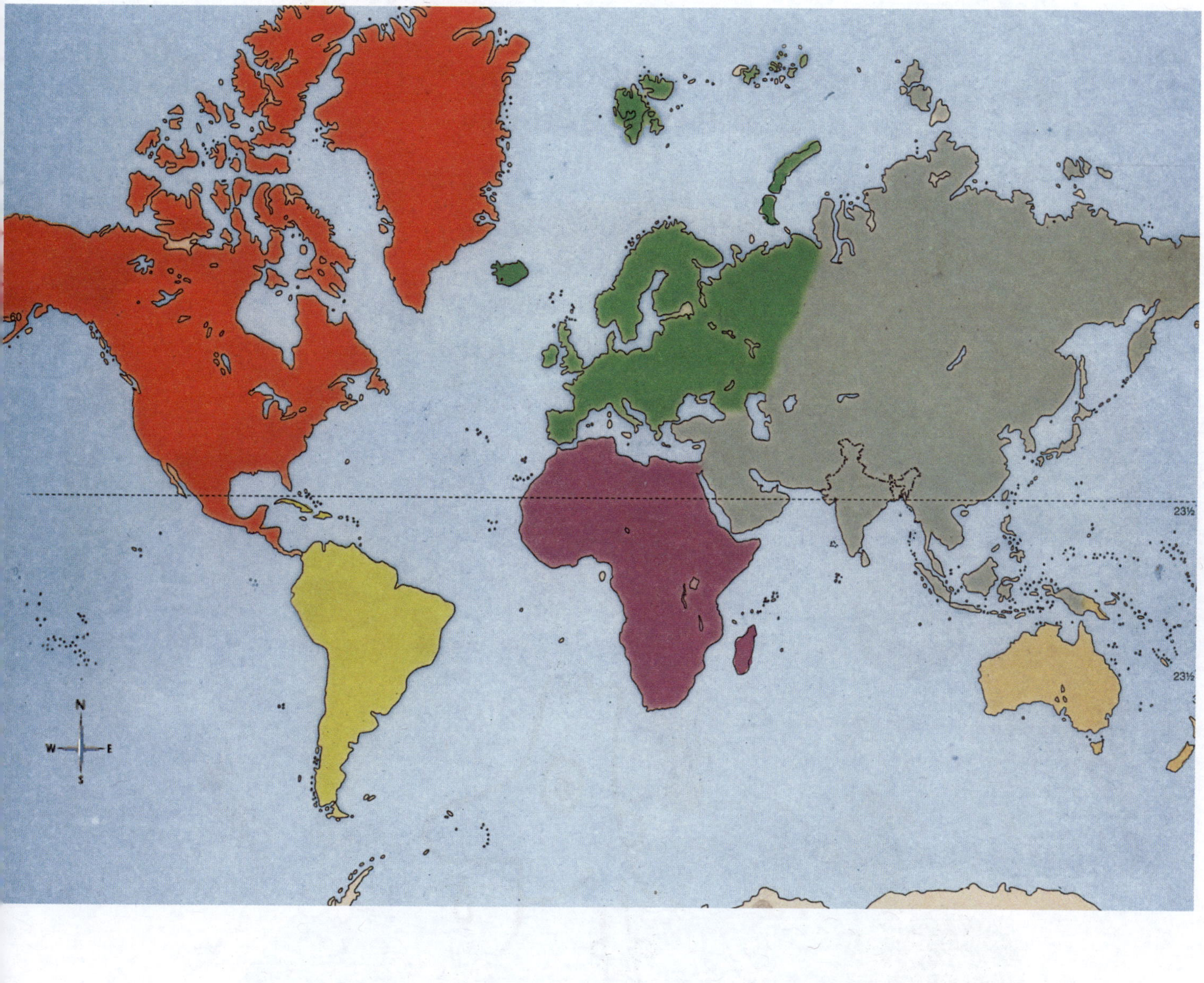

60
23½
23½
N
W
E
S

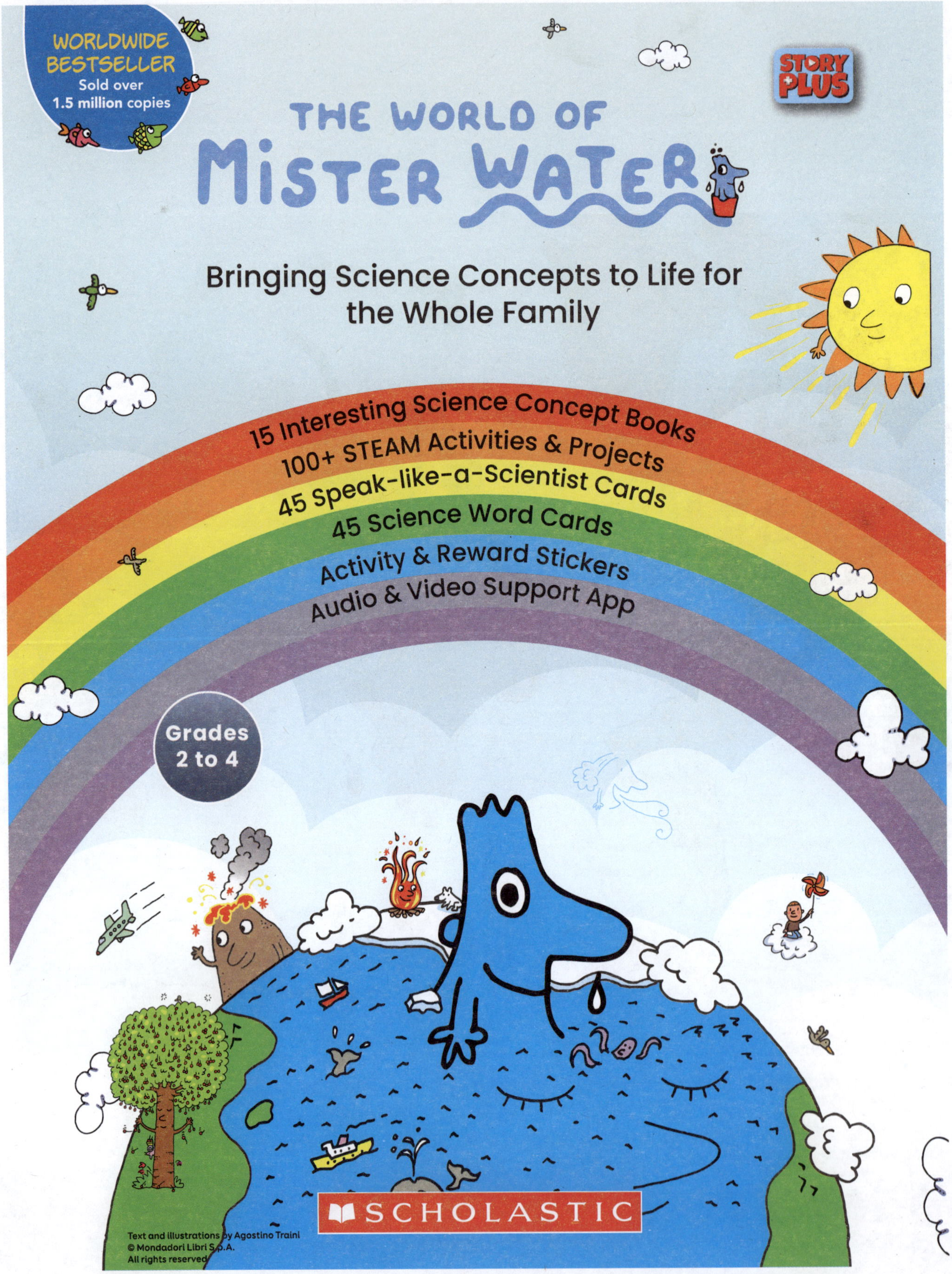
WORLDWIDE BESTSELLER
Sold over 1.5 million copies
STORY PLUS
THE WORLD OF MISTER WATER
Bringing Science Concepts to Life for the Whole Family
15 Interesting Science Concept Books
100+ STEAM Activities & Projects
45 Speak-like-a-Scientist Cards
45 Science Word Cards
Activity & Reward Stickers
Audio & Video Support App
Grades 2 to 4
SCHOLASTIC
Text and illustrations by Agostino Traini
© Mondadori Libri S.p.A.
All rights reserved